A WAR BRIDE'S STORY

Risking it all for Love After World War II

ROMANCE/HISTORY

by Cynthia J. Faryon

PUBLISHED BY ALTITUDE PUBLISHING CANADA LTD.
1500 Railway Avenue, Canmore, Alberta T1W 1P6
www.altitudepublishing.com
1-800-957-6888

Extreme care has been taken to ensure that all information presented in this book is accurate and up to date. Neither the author nor the publisher can be held responsible for any errors.

Publisher	Stephen Hutchings
Associate Publisher	Kara Turner
Series Editor	Jill Foran
Digital photo colouring	Scott Manktelow

We acknowledge the financial support of the Government of Canada through the Book Publishing Industry Development Program (BPIDP) for our publishing activities.

Altitude GreenTree Program
Altitude Publishing will plant twice as many trees as were used in the manufacturing of this product.

National Library of Canada Cataloguing in Publication Data

Faryon, Cynthia J., 1956-
A war bride's story / Cynthia J. Faryon

(Amazing stories)
Includes bibliographical references.
ISBN 1-55153-959-4

1. Cramer, Gwen. 2. War brides--Canada--Biography. 3. Farm life--Saskatchewan--Arborfield. 4. Arborfield (Sask.)--Biography. I. Title. II. Series: Amazing stories (Canmore, Alta.)

FC3549.A72Z49 2004   971.24'203'092   C2003-907173-1

An application for the trademark for Amazing Stories™ has been made and the registered trademark is pending.

Printed and bound in Canada by Friesens
2 4 6 8 9 7 5 3 1

Cover: Gwen around the time she left England for a new life in Canada
All photographs are from Gwen Cramer's collection.

A WAR BRIDE'S STORY

To my mother, and to all the war brides who came bravely to this land.

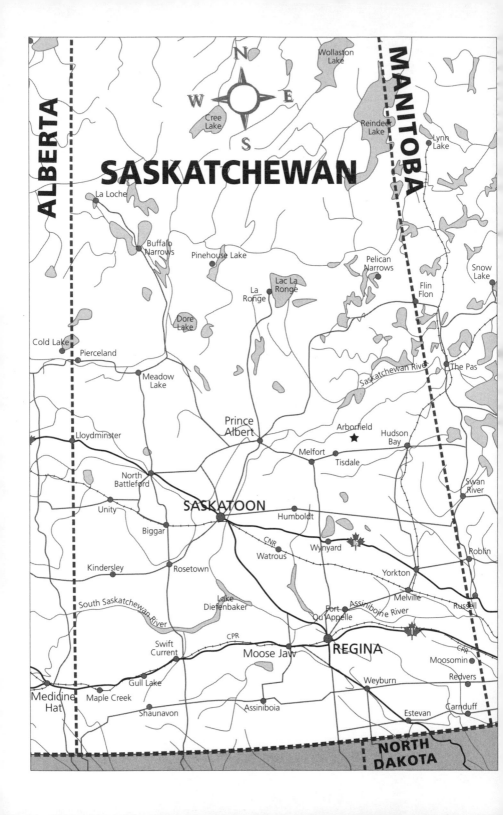

Contents

Prologue

The ship's whistle blows a long blast, followed by two short. Even though it's only four in the morning, and the sky is black over the liquid lead swells of the Atlantic, I get up. Conscious this will be one of the few days left when I'll be permitted to wear the uniform of Air Force blue, I reverently button the large gold orbs, place my officer's cap at the rakish angle of a Canadian flyboy, and shrug into my greatcoat. The coat hangs loosely over the uniform, helping to hide my thin frame; bulk seems to be missing from my ribs, and I smile when I think of what Ma will say when she sees me so skinny. Gwen, my wife, is a great cook, but war rations made mealtime a struggle. And while there was always plenty to eat at the mess hall, 38 missions as a rear gunner robbed me of my healthy appetite. I feel 75, not 25.

Silently, I join other dark figures along the ship's rail. United in war, we are now strangers in peace, and stand soberly hunched together, gazing ahead into the darkness towards the direction of home. None of us knows what to expect. Soon we'll be with family again, we'll return to where we grew up, yet everything will feel different.

"Just like a picture I once saw in a magazine, of POWs standing wordlessly along a stretch of barbed wire fence, shoulders touching, just staring." The sound of my own voice breaks the stillness, and although it is nothing more than a whisper, it echoes loudly around us.

"Funny that," the man next to me says quietly. "I was thinking that very thing."

I turn and smile at him, realizing this man, who has been closer to me than my brother during our time in the service, was becoming a stranger now that the war is over. If I can feel this way about him, how will I feel about Ma and Pa, or worse, how will I react to Gwen when she arrives from England?

I think of my wife, pregnant with my child, patiently waiting to follow me here, and I feel guilt. We were young, scared, and in love. Two complete strangers thrown together by the world at war, with nothing in common but the need to survive. Here I am going home and feeling out of place, but how will she feel when it's her turn to cross the Atlantic? Will we still be in love? We had lived for living's sake, but neither of us had looked beyond surviving the war.

Suddenly, I catch my first glimpse of land and realize that this moment, this instant, is what I had longed

*for every time I felt the Halifax Bomber leave the earth.
This dreamlike homecoming is what I had envisioned
with every round of ammunition I fired, every plane I
saw explode, and every load of bombs I dropped. I had
thought of it a thousand times, dreamed of it at night,
and now I am full of emotion and I can't begin to find
release. I am more terrified of this — my last journey —
than any mission I flew over Germany.*

*No one is there to meet me when the ship docks in
Halifax. And no one greets me at any of the train stations
along the way home to Saskatchewan. I stare out the
windows of the passenger car and watch the monotonous
lines of fences, beginning nowhere and ending nowhere.
Nothing has changed. The telephone poles still stand gar-
ishly, the land is still flat, and the sky is still huge.*

*When I reach Arborfield, the whole damn town is
there to greet me and the other hometown boys who had
gone off to fight. Those of us stepping onto the platform
are welcomed with banners, hugs, tears, and music. With
tears in my eyes and a lump in my throat, I hug Ma so
hard I almost break a rib.*

*Again I realize that nothing has changed:
Arborfield, the farm, the people — everything is as I left it.
The only thing that has changed, it seems, is me. A life-
time ago, I left here a boy going off to war to find glory
and honour, and to earn the respect of my family and*

friends. Now I return, a married man with a child on the way.

Soon my wife, my very English wife, who looks like a porcelain doll and wears high-heeled shoes, will leave her home and join me here in Arborfield. I wonder what she'll think of my hometown, with its board sidewalks, mud streets, and piles of horse manure steaming in the snow. I smile as I try to picture her in overalls under the belly of a cow, a bucket between her knees.

"My God, Gwen," I say to no one in particular. "We survived the war, but will you survive Canada?"

Chapter 1
War

On September 1, 1939, Hitler's army crossed into Polish territory, and the German Air Force bombed Warsaw. The German invasion had begun. Months of threats had come to an end; the gauntlet for war had been thrown.

In Golders Green, a community on the outskirts of London, England, people tried to go about their usual routines. The morning of September 3, 1939, began like most September mornings. The suburban gardens smelled of impending autumn, the birds were singing their usual songs, and 17-year-old Gwendoline Haskell was contentedly helping her Aunt Ivy with her sewing in the sitting room of their small bungalow. The two women went about their tasks in quiet comfort, and Gwen, once again, thought about how lucky she was.

Gwen's life hadn't always been happy and serene. In the 1920s, her parents divorced and abandoned her and her sister, Joan, to an orphanage. Not long after the girls arrived there, Joan was adopted, and Gwen never saw her again. After spending a few years in the orphanage, Gwen went to live with her prosperous Uncle Norman and Aunt Ivy, and was given the chance to enjoy all the finer things in life. Growing up, she took dance and elocution lessons, and attended the ballet and the theatre. Her favourite pastimes included visiting the zoo and listening to the bands playing in the park. The only mar on her comfortable life was the heartache that came from missing her sister.

As Gwen and her Aunt Ivy continued to stitch, a piercing wail penetrated the air, sending shivers of dread down Gwen's spine. "An air raid siren," she thought to herself as she stared at Ivy's shocked face. "Planes are coming, with bombs to kill us."

Suddenly, an unfamiliar fear gripped Gwen's body. She thought of her Uncle Norman, who was at work in London, and said a silent prayer for his safety. Then, realizing she and Ivy needed to get to the closest air-raid shelter, Gwen dropped her sewing and rushed to grab her most essential belongings. She ran into her bedroom, but on the verge of panic, couldn't decide what to take with her to the shelter. Finally, she grabbed her journal off the bed and hurried into the hall, where her aunt was waiting for her. Ivy was holding a teapot. The two women looked at one another and Gwen realized that her strong and capable aunt was as afraid as she was.

Ivy and Gwen left the house, joining the rest of their neighbours as they made their way to the nearby air-raid shelter. People were staggering to the shelter in various degrees of shock, carrying blankets, chairs, and other creature comforts they thought to bring with them at the last moment. Like Ivy, some people had simply grabbed what had been within easy reach. They clutched items like pictures, hairbrushes, and books.

The municipal shelter, which was located in the basement of a house, was sectioned into three rooms with two long corridors between them. The inside walls were lined with corrugated steel that was propped into place with beams of timber. Beer bottles filled with fresh drinking water were stacked in every corner of the shelter, and makeshift latrines were located behind a couple piles of sacks.

When Gwen and Ivy entered the main room of the air-raid shelter, they saw that everyone would have to sit very close to one another. Neighbours crowded together, shoulders touching in the dark, drawing comfort in the proximity of others as they faced their own nightmares. The smell of nervous sweat permeated the stuffy room. Sitting in the dim light, Gwen was acutely aware of the other bodies, all damp with perspiration. Ordinarily she would have found the situation repugnant. Now, however, she found it oddly comforting.

There was a hush in the shelter as everyone waited for the first sounds of bombs falling. They waited all day and throughout the night. Finally, in the early morning hours, the all clear sounded; people gathered their items of comfort and made their way back to their homes, wondering what the near future would bring.

Emerging from the shelter after a night of waiting was a surreal experience for Gwen. It took a few moments for her eyes to adjust to the sunlight, and even more time for her mind to catch up with the reality that the country was at war. The landscape of Golders Green hadn't changed; birds were still singing, the sun was warm, and a soft breeze blew the leaves on the trees. To Gwen, however, the world had turned upside down overnight.

Exhausted, Gwen and Ivy walked back to their little bungalow — Gwen still clutching her journal, Ivy her teapot. When they got home, Gwen returned the journal to its hiding place at the foot of her bed, and Ivy washed out the teapot and made tea.

War

As they sipped their tea and ate biscuits, the two women listened to the radio and heard the devastating news they already knew was coming: Britain had declared war on Germany. The biscuits tasted like sawdust after that, and Gwen looked at her Aunt Ivy with tears in her eyes.

India joined with England against Germany and the Third Reich, and Australia and New Zealand quickly followed. On September 6, 1939, South Africa joined the Allied forces, and Canada followed on September 10.

Soon, houses in small villages throughout England, especially those close to the English Channel, were issued bomb shelters. The indoor shelters, called Morrison shelters, were made of thick steel with sprung bottoms and caged sides. The Anderson shelters were similarly made, but were used outdoors, their ends buried in the ground for stability.

Gas masks were handed out to the public, and people were instructed to put sticky paper over their windows to prevent injury in case the glass was blown out in an explosion. Heavy blackout curtains were also hung in every window, and lanterns on all vehicles were disconnected. The grim realities of war had crept into the English way of life.

To Gwen, it seemed the world had truly gone mad. Her family, such as it was, was being split apart. Her male cousins all joined up to fight across the channel, and every available civilian joined a volunteer group to help the troops.

At night, the whirr of German planes, the whistles of dropping explosives, and the distant sound of exploding bombs serenaded the people of England as they tried to sleep. Adding to this symphony was the frequent sound of air raid sirens, which would summon people out of bed and into their shelters.

Emerging from these shelters after a night of bombing was an awful and eerie experience for Gwen. Each morning, smoke and dust from mortar and brick filled the air, dancing discordantly in the daylight's sunbeams. It always took a few moments for Gwen's eyes to adjust to the sunlight and her mind to catch up with the destruction. But perhaps the worst part of these dreamlike mornings was the smell; the acrid sting of burned fuel, TNT, and dust that clung in cloying determination to her olfactory senses.

Most days, Gwen found her way home in a daze, stepping carefully over the countless broken bricks that had been flung into the streets from the blasts, and hurrying to find out if her aunt and uncle's bungalow was still intact. She would stop only if there was a fire burning; when a home in the neighbourhood was in flames, everyone became a firefighter. Bucket brigades were formed, and sacks and shovels of dirt — and whatever else was handy — were hurled into the flames. Battling the fires gave the public something tangible to fight. Though it didn't completely end the feelings of helplessness, it gave most people a focus for their anger and fear.

A year after the fighting began, Gwen was told she would need to find some war work to do. She and Ivy had just returned from North Devon. They had left London to escape the raids, but after only a few weeks of being away, they'd realized they missed Norman and their comfortable house too much, and had gone home. Due to her asthma, Gwen found she wasn't able to work in the Women's Land Army or the Women's Army Corps, so Uncle Norman suggested she volunteer at the Air Ministry in Adastral house in London. He thought the work would help his niece cope. All of England was under siege, and young Gwen had never felt more vulnerable.

After a period of settling in, Gwen found she enjoyed her contribution to the war effort. She especially enjoyed the new friendships she forged with the other girls in her office. Before she knew it, four years had passed, and the war had become a part of her life.

The girls in the office often chatted and exchanged stories of romantic meetings with military men. They pulled the files of the servicemen they were dating, checking the soldiers' backgrounds to ensure they were not being lied to. They giggled over their tea and biscuits, comparing notes and indulging in war gossip.

Although the paperwork at the Air Ministry was easy, the bombing raids continued to make life challenging. After a nine-hour shift at the ministry, and two hours of commuting, by the time Gwen's train pulled into her station at 11 p.m. she was too worn out for anything but tea and bed. Her exhaustion from this gruelling schedule was further aggravated by the strict food rations in place, and by the blackout restrictions, which forced her to travel home at night in the pitch black.

At the end of the working week, if the threat of air raids was minimal, Gwen sometimes accompanied her friends to a local club or show. One of their favourite places was the Review, held in the Windmill Theatre, where talented dancers, singers, and entertainers performed regularly for the troops. They didn't serve liquor there, although it was occasionally smuggled in.

Gwen and her friends also enjoyed the local pub across from the theatre — until a German bomb demolished it. There were many deaths in the bombing, and Gwen knew a number of the people killed. Some of them were dancers from the theatre.

During the last weekend of November 1943, a Canadian girlfriend phoned Gwen up and invited her to the movies. When they arrived at the theatre, the two friends discovered they had already seen the movie, so they went to the club next door for some dancing.

The club was packed, and loud music filled the room. Soon after the girls entered, two Canadian flyboys approached them and asked them to dance. Smiling into the face of Pilot Officer Larry Cramer, Gwen noticed at once how handsome he was, and quickly accepted his invitation. Larry danced liked a dream. He smelled of Canadian cigarettes, and spoke slowly and shyly. As the evening wore on, it became apparent that Larry found Gwen as fascinating as she found him. They danced, laughed, and talked all night.

He told her he was born in a part of Canada called Saskatchewan, where his parents owned and operated a mixed farm just outside a small town called Arborfield. He said it was a very different lifestyle there, slower and more relaxed. He also confessed that he found England strange and foreign. Gwen listened intently to this handsome man, and soon found herself thinking that she would love to visit the place he was from. He seemed genuine and soft spoken, with a wonderful sense of humour.

Larry smiled at Gwen and said he found her very beautiful. She laughed and told him not to string her a line, as she had heard that one before. She also said that she would verify any stories he told her through his records at the Air Ministry office. He chuckled, and then proceeded to tell her tales so tall that she was shocked at his nerve. Gwen knew he was only trying to see if she was interested enough to look him up in the ministry files. She was.

On February 22, 1944, just 11 weeks after they met, Gwen and Larry were married in a London registry office. Though it was wartime and ration vouchers were hard to come by, Gwen's aunt and uncle made sure the wedding was done in style. They hired a Bentley with a chauffeur to drive the bride and groom, and held a small reception to celebrate. Larry's aircrew from Elvington Air Base in Yorkshire all came down in force.

Larry and Gwen spent their honeymoon at the Ritz Hotel in London. Feeling skittish and nervous, Gwen had signed her maiden name, Haskell, at the front desk instead of her married name of Cramer. The desk clerk had immediately noticed the name difference and had frowned disapprovingly. From then on, the staff treated the newlyweds as though they were living in sin. A few days later, tired of the stern looks, Gwen left the large marriage certificate on the hotel dresser for the chambermaid to see. This didn't seem to make too much difference, but Gwen felt better.

On February 28, the last night of their honeymoon,

Larry photographed in 1944

Gwen and Larry were treated to a night of unwelcome fireworks when German bombers swept the London skies. The air raid sirens screamed, bombs whistled as they dropped from their planes, and the sounds of shattering explosions could be heard in the distance. Tired of the war and resenting the intrusion, Larry and Gwen pulled their blankets and pillows into their hotel room closet for the night, deciding not go to the shelter.

Gwen curled up with her new husband, and prayed her family would be kept safe.

Chapter 2
Larry Goes Home

he next year flew by. Larry, now a married man, was given leave to live off the base. He and Gwen found a small house in North York, an area within easy travelling distance to Elvington so that Larry could be called in at a moment's notice. He was finishing his tour of duty, and had been notified that he would be appointed liaison officer to the Free French Forces, and would spend the next year instructing.

The Rudge 500 motorbike Larry bought from the skipper of his bomber crew provided a great deal of freedom and entertainment for the newlyweds during their first year together. At first, Larry had to convince Gwen it was safe for them to ride it. She was hesitant because the regulations for living off base stipulated that Larry needed to be near a telephone while on standby. However, after ripping up the Yorkshire roads and feeling the wind whipping through her hair during their first ride, she was game for more.

During one particular motorbike outing, Larry pulled up to see if his swerving and speed had frightened her. Looking over his shoulder, expecting to see Gwen's face white with fear, he was surprised to see that his beautiful wife was smiling from ear to ear. She looked somewhat comical under her rollers and scarf — she had just done her hair when Larry had convinced her to take a ride.

"Larry, could I have a crack at it?" she asked, eyes sparkling.

"What, you mean — drive it?" He was shocked.

"Yes, you ninny. You aren't afraid of me driving it are you?"

So, off they went. Gwen drove wildly, scarf to the wind, rollers flying, her hair in Larry's eyes. Suddenly, the bike veered to the left, then to the right, and before Larry realized what was happening, they'd bounced over a ditch, bumped along a field, skidded to a stop, and ended up in a heap on the grass.

Gwen, red in the face, a pink roller dangling over

one eye, coughed and giggled. As tears of laughter streamed down her cheeks she sputtered, "I breathed in a bloody fly!" They both laughed harder. Then, with a twinkle in her eye, Gwen said, "Do you suppose the extra protein would be good for the baby?"

Larry looked at his wife in disbelief. Gwen patted her tummy and nodded her head. Her gentle affirmation brought a wide, joyful smile to his face — among all this death and destruction, he was going to be a father.

That night, as Gwen and Larry were lying in bed and drifting off to sleep, they were awakened by the sickening, nasal sound of a German buzz bomb. They heard it at the same time, and both knew there was nowhere to run; the missile was above them, and much too close for them to escape. In the dark, Gwen reached for Larry's hand and clutched his fingers. Larry held hers tightly, then pulled her to him as the tinny, rasping sound got closer. The frightened pair held their breath, waiting for the missile's engine to cut out.

Larry had seen Allied fighters actually tip these missiles over in mid-flight, and then send them back over the channel to meet the Germans. As he listened, he wished one of those fighters would rescue them now, but it seemed more than unlikely; all he could hear was the ominous buzzing of the missile above their home. Hugging Gwen as hard as he could, Larry felt in his gut that their time had come.

"Cuddle up, Gwen," he whispered, hoping she could not hear the terror in his voice. "We can't fight this one. He's too close."

Larry could feel the swell of Gwen's stomach against his own. He closed his eyes and thought of his unborn child. As if she could read his mind, Gwen whispered, "We'll never see our baby." Then she began to cry softly.

Suddenly, the buzzing sound was replaced by a shrieking noise as the bomb descended quickly from above. Gwen and Larry held each other tightly and began to pray.

The explosion that followed shook the house, blowing out windows and cracking walls. But somehow, the bomb had missed them. Their house, perched on the hill above a river valley, was still intact. The missile had dropped right past them and had landed in the valley below, in an area known as Hampstead.

Gwen and Larry left their bed and ran down the hill to see if they could help. Fire was everywhere, and several were homes destroyed. Among the casualties were a number of Jewish people new to the area, children among them. They had recently escaped Germany and found refuge on Britain's soil.

"Oh, Larry," Gwen said quietly as she surveyed the heartbreaking scene. "Oh, Larry…"

Larry Goes Home

* * *

In January of 1945, Larry was granted a few days leave to spend with his wife. These were to be their final days together before he was shipped home. Larry had been grounded months before, and was soon to be repatriated to Canada. Gwen, however, could not go with him. She had to follow at another date, after the baby was born and the proper paperwork had been completed and filed. Gwen and Larry had been married almost a year then, and the baby was due in May.

Larry left for Canada in April of 1945. Mark Lawrence Cramer was born one month later, on May 23, 1945. Larry missed meeting his son by only a few short weeks.

With Larry gone, the months dragged on for Gwen. She was a married woman with a child, yet she was without her husband. Giving up her home in North York, she and Mark moved back into her aunt and uncle's bungalow in Golders Green.

A year later, in March of 1946, a long awaited telegram arrived informing Gwen that she and Mark had been cleared to leave England from Liverpool, and sail to Canada on the RMS *Mauritania*, which would dock in Halifax, Nova Scotia.

The telegram assured Gwen that as a war bride, she

would be looked after from the beginning to the end of her voyage. Transporting the war brides was the responsibility of the Department of National Defence, the Canadian Red Cross, and the immigration branch of the Canadian Department of Energy, Mines, and Resources. The Canadian Wives Bureau arranged for Gwen and Mark's passage, and would deliver them to the ships, distribute information, and assign them to Red Cross officials, who would look after their daily needs.

When it came time to depart for Liverpool, Gwen said her farewells to family and friends. After settling in the transport bus, she watched sadly as her aunt and uncle stood on the street, waving goodbye. She wondered if she would ever see them again.

The transport bus took Gwen and Mark to a local church hall, where many other war brides waited with their own children — over 900 would be travelling on the ship to Halifax. The next morning, after a fitful sleep in a room filled with restless children and emotional women, they boarded a train for Liverpool.

The RMS *Mauritania* stood ominously at the dock in Liverpool. It was a troop ship, but it had been re-equipped with extra bathroom facilities for transporting the women and children.

Gwen and Mark shared a cabin with three other English war brides. One was pregnant, and spent the trip throwing up or sleeping; the other two each had a young child. At the beginning of the journey, many of the women — including Gwen — were simply too seasick to move around or even eat. However, once Gwen's stomach became accustomed to the motion of the boat, she found the food onboard delicious. After years of war rations, the white bread rolls, real eggs, crisp bacon, and fresh oranges were wonderful treats. The first trip to the dining room was a feast for the senses, and Gwen stood there for a moment savouring the smells and sights before her.

Some of the other women had tears in their eyes the first time they saw the food being served. The brides most affected by the delicious spread before them were those from continental Europe, where many had suffered starvation. Looking at these women, Gwen was reminded that as hard as the war had been on England, it had been much more devastating in other countries.

In the evenings, the brides mingled with the rest of the travellers and crew onboard the RMS *Mauritania*. They talked about their new homes, as well as the homes and family they were leaving behind. They watched movies and danced to live music, which was always accompanied by the sound of crying babies, the smell of diapers, and the swaying of the ship beneath their feet. The distractions were welcomed, as they helped alleviate some of the women's anxiety over what to expect in their new county.

The RMS *Mauritania* also had a few troops onboard, and these men helped where they could with the children, and with the brides who were too seasick to be left alone. Gwen had many conversations with the troops about Canada and what to expect. One serviceman laughed when she told him she was going to live in her husband's hometown in northern Saskatchewan. He told her he hoped she liked snow and enjoyed mud.

The Canadian coast finally came into sight on the twelfth day of the journey from England. Gwen stood eagerly at the ship's rail with the other brides, all of them straining to catch a glimpse of their new home.

By the time the RMS *Mauritania* finished docking in Halifax, the icy March wind was blowing ruthlessly. Gwen snuggled Mark close to keep him warm, shocked at how the cold air penetrated every layer of clothing she was wearing. England had never been this cold, and though her coat had always provided more than adequate protection against a blast of ocean air back home, it could now barely keep the chill at bay.

Standing on deck as instructed, Gwen felt forlorn and unsure of herself. Mark, now an active 10-month-old, struggled in her arms, squirming to be set free. Gwen ignored her son's protests and cuddled him closer, realizing yet again that in a few short days, father and son would meet for the first time.

While she held Mark in one arm, Gwen gripped their landing cards tightly in her other hand, fingers white from nerves as much as from the cold. She worried about meeting her new family and felt anxious to get started on the next leg of the journey. Her luggage was piled high on the deck behind her under the letter "C" for her surname, "Cramer." Around her were hundreds of others, all waiting impatiently for help to disembark. Not for the first time, Gwen felt a pang of loss as she thought of her family back in England.

Soon, all the war brides made their way off the ship to the pier below — Pier 21, where so many had landed before. During and immediately following World War II, thousands of war brides entered Canada through this portal. All stood on the decks of various ships feeling the same homesickness, hoping for a happy future in their new country.

As Gwen stood on the pier with the others, she gazed across to the shoreline at the bleak scene that welcomed them. Canada looked stark and felt cold; even the people hugging and yelling greetings couldn't ease her mounting anxiety. She knew she would not relax until she was home, wherever — and whatever — that turned out to be.

All the war brides were appointed two soldiers in uniform, one to help them off the boat with the children, and the other to tend to their luggage. Then each woman was directed to the main dispersal point, which was housed in a large warehouse. There was a band playing on the dock, and people were waving and shouting, welcoming them all to Canada. Some fortunate war brides were greeted warmly by husbands and members of their new families; others stood by forlornly, waiting for more travelling into the vast unknown.

Gwen and Mark waited for someone to tell them where to go next. Still gripping her papers, Gwen watched silently as her luggage was piled close to the dispersal hall for loading onto the train once she had been cleared.

The Red Cross volunteers hustled the groups together. The women and children were ushered into the big main hall, where they were told to check the bulletin board for messages then join the line with their papers, ready to satisfy customs and obtain travel permits.

Gwen hungrily scanned the bulletin board for a familiar name and smiled when she read hers. Larry had sent her a telegram. It read: "I will be waiting for you both in Saskatoon, and we'll spend a couple of days there just the three of us. Ma and Pa are waiting anxiously, and looking forward to welcoming you both home. I miss you. I love you. See you soon."

Seeing the note pinned on the board brought tears to Gwen's eyes. If she was ever unsure of her future in this new country, she now knew her husband was worth the effort of leaving home. Impatient to be reunited with Larry, Gwen asked one of the attendants how many hours it would take to get to Saskatoon.

"Three days ma'am," he answered.

Gwen sighed and fought back fresh tears of exhaustion and disappointment. She had made it to Canada, and now she wanted her husband's arms around her. Three days felt like three years.

Suddenly, one of the war brides standing nearby burst into tears. Her husband had posted a telegram that said he had made a huge mistake in marrying her and told her to return to England, as she was not welcome in his home. As the woman cried uncontrollably, her two-year-old child looking confused, Gwen swallowed a lump in her throat. For the first time, she realized just how big a chance she had taken in travelling to Canada. She loved her husband, but they had been apart for over a year. It had never occurred to her that he might have second thoughts. But for the grace of God, she could have been in that woman's shoes.

Gwen continued to clutch her son in bone-weary

arms, surveying her new country as she stood in line. She could see the landscape through the windows of the hall, or at least what was visible through the sea mist. Tears flowed freely down her wind-bitten cheeks as she thought of England. A few weeks earlier, the English countryside had been in the first blooms of spring. Just days before she had left her home, Gwen had gone for a walk and had gathered purple wood violets. The English forest had thrown a canopy of green above her head as she had wandered; robins had called from tree to tree, and nearby a brook had bubbled and giggled over the rocks, feeding a shallow pond. She'd dangled her feet in the water, and had breathed in the scent of the English country.

When Gwen had arrived home from her walk, her aunt had served tea on fine English bone china. They had munched on biscuits and chatted about nothing in particular. Auntie had reminded her to cross her legs at the ankle and sit up straight, and, even though Gwen was 24, a mother and a wife, she had done as she was told. After tea, Gwen had arranged the violets in a small Waterford vase and had left them on Aunt Ivy's bureau in the front bedroom. The vase had a handmade lace runner to protect the dark well-oiled oak top.

Closing her eyes to the sights around her, and her mind to her place in line, Gwen could almost smell those violets still. The flowers would be in the trash by now, and Gwen wondered if she would ever walk the English countryside again.

England was far away, and as the wild Atlantic waves pounded at the Nova Scotia shore, Gwen tried to stem her renewed feelings of homesickness. She continued to look out at the landscape, noticing grimly that the heavy sea mist had turned everything into a dull grey. Even the trees stood stark and barren against the sky. Their roots clung to round cold rocks, sucking at the salt water and struggling against the wind. This landscape seemed ominous to Gwen in comparison to the lovely wooded neighbourhood back in England. She had known Canada would be different, but she was unprepared for just how different. She wanted to go home, and if not for the words of love on Larry's telegram, she would have broken down and begged to be booked on the next voyage to England.

While Gwen was waiting for her travelling papers, a Red Cross volunteer gave Mark a cup of juice and a cookie, then offered her a cup of tea. The tea was strong, bitter, and laced with milk and sugar. No doubt it had been hot at one time, but now in cold fingers, the drink was lukewarm.

Leaving the pier at last, Gwen and Mark were hustled onto a CN train that was to pass through New

Brunswick, Quebec, and Ontario. Gwen found this part of the trip wonderful; she loved watching the brides getting off at various stops along the way. She laughed quietly at all the nervous men and anxious new in-laws lining up at the stations with flowers, corsages, and uncertain smiles.

Finally, the train stopped at a station in a city called Winnipeg, where she and Mark were to change trains. In his last letter, Larry had referred to Winnipeg as "Winterpeg," and upon her arrival in that town along the river, she had to agree with his assessment. She had never seen so much snow in her life! People were skating on the frozen river at a place referred to as "The Forks." They were bundled up, scarves around their necks and mouths, and though it was a bright day, it looked much too cold to tempt Gwen from the warm confines of the train.

A sergeant from the Canadian army came onboard, greeted Gwen, and offered to take Mark for her. She smiled at him. He smiled back, then guided her off the train and showed her to a waiting room full of people. Gwen assumed they were all there to catch the same CP train that she and Mark were waiting for. She was slightly taken aback when all of these smiling people came up to shake her hand. A moment later, someone laughingly explained that they were all cousins and relatives of

Larry's; they had come to welcome her since he couldn't be there. Gwen, so overcome with gratitude, started to cry yet again.

An hour or so later, the soldier helped Gwen find her place on the next train, giving both her and Mark a hug before he left. Gwen, not sure how to react, did what most English do when bellboys and desk clerks lend a hand: she tried to tip him. The soldier laughed and told her that he was actually Larry's uncle, and that tipping was not a family tradition.

During the final leg of the trip, Mark was a good little traveller. He played, laughed, ate, and slept all the way across Manitoba to Saskatoon, Saskatchewan. While he slept, Gwen spent a good deal of time looking out the window at the winter landscape. Mile after mile of fence posts stuck like brown lumps out of the snow. Every once in a while, a chicken coop, a poorly painted farmhouse, or a pile of hay would appear on the clean, white fields. Cattle chewed their feed and watched silently as the train went by, and now and again, a hawk circled in the huge canopy of blue.

Pretty, Gwen thought to herself as she shivered — pretty flat, pretty cold, pretty deserted.

Chapter 3
Oh Canada!

arry, looking handsome in civilian clothes, was waiting for his wife and son at the Saskatoon station. Gwen cried when she saw him. He kissed her as if he would never stop, until Mark screamed and tried to push him away. Mark wasn't happy to see this tall stranger hugging his mother. He started to yell so loud that everyone within earshot knew how outraged he really was.

Once Mark settled down, the small family walked a short distance to the hotel. On the way, Gwen was surprised at all the food she saw displayed in the stores. Her first dinner with her husband and son was steak, potatoes, and carrots, served at the hotel. Sharing a banana

split with Mark for dessert, she began to feel that perhaps Canada was all right after all.

After spending a couple of days in Saskatoon, Larry
was anxious to get his wife and child home. He had
informed Gwen that they would be staying with his parents on the family homestead, but promised they would
only be there for a month — until he could finish fixing
up their house in town. Gwen and Larry purchased their
tickets to Arborfield and left on the early morning train.
As they boarded, Larry warned his wife that life on the
farm wouldn't be a picnic. Gwen smiled to herself; she
was with her handsome husband and wonderful son,
how bad could it really be?

Larry then told her they would be on the train until
midnight — and what a train it was. There were no proper seats onboard, just wooden benches. Try as she
might, Gwen could not get comfortable on the hard sur-
face, and the clickety clack of the metal wheels on metal
tracks made such a racket that she felt she'd go insane.
Mark wouldn't sleep, and crawled persistently on the
dirty floor. Larry, however, lay stretched out on a bench,
snoring contentedly. As he slept, Gwen's anxiety over
meeting her in-laws increased with every kilometre
travelled. Unable to sit down any longer, she woke Larry
up, handed Mark to him, and announced she was off to
find the facilities.

Gwen reached the end of the car and passed through to the next. She knew her in-laws would be at the station to meet the train, and she wanted to freshen up. A kind conductor pointed to a door at the end of the car that led to a washroom the size of a very small closet. Once inside the washroom, Gwen shut the door, and was barely able to turn around. She wondered if there was a larger washroom elsewhere, as she couldn't imagine her husband fitting in this one.

Sitting down, she saw a sign directly opposite her. It read: "PLEASE DO NOT FLUSH TOILET WHEN STOPPED AT THE STATION." Odd sign, she thought. Gwen washed her hands and then fixed her hair, using the tiny mirror on the wall. Ready to leave, she pulled the chain above her head to flush the toilet. There was a noisy rush of air, and then the bowl emptied right onto the track. Shocked, Gwen stared through the toilet hole at the ground passing below the train. She couldn't believe her waste had just been flushed out of the train and into plain view!

Gwen stormed back to the car, embarrassed and disgusted. She told Larry what a horrible little contraption the toilet was, proclaiming it utterly uncivilized to flush bodily waste out onto the track where everyone could see it. Larry laughed, which made her more indignant. She vowed she would not go to the washroom again until they arrived somewhere with more dignified facilities.

At midnight, as the train slowed and approached the Arborfield station, Gwen prepared to meet her husband's family for the first time. She smoothed her red silk dress, pinched her cheeks to add colour, and reapplied her red lipstick. Patting her hair into place, she asked Larry if she was presentable. She could see the lights on at the small station in the distance, and noticed several people standing out in the snow. Her stomach began doing flip-flops.

Even though there had been snow on the ground when they had left Saskatoon that morning, Gwen had chosen to wear open-toed high heels for her journey. Now, as the train pulled to a stop, she noticed that all of the people on the platform were dressed for winter. Suddenly, Gwen felt overdressed socially, and underdressed for practical purposes. She looked nervously at her husband. She wanted to make a good impression, but what would these strangers think of her when she slipped and slid through the muck on the platform, then slogged through knee-deep snow to the motorcar in silly shoes?

Larry placed his arm around her and gave her a squeeze and a quick kiss on the cheek. Meanwhile, a man and a woman with smiles on their faces boarded the train and came down the aisle towards them. Gwen's heart began to race as she watched the couple approach — she could not help but stare at the odd-looking pair.

The man, who's crooked grin revealed he was missing a couple of teeth, had a hand-carved wooden pipe sticking out of the side of his mouth. The pipe didn't appear to be lit. He was dressed for the elements, wearing a well-patched pair of work pants, a woollen curler's cap, gumboots that had seen better days, and a Hudson's Bay coat that hung limply on his tall, thin frame. The woman was wearing mittens, a blue print dress under a threadbare wool coat, and a pair of men's boots. On her head was a toque pulled down so low that it almost covered her eyes. Her salt and pepper hair, damp from the weather, stuck out haphazardly from under the hat.

Gwen swallowed and looked to Larry; she was hoping these people weren't his parents. But Larry handed Mark over to the woman, and after a moment had passed, he introduced his wife to his Ma and Pa.

Ma looked at Gwen from head to toe, and judging by the critical expression on her face, Gwen knew Ma's first impression of her wasn't a good one. Ma's frown deepened when her eyes rested on her new daughter-in-law's face. As Gwen stared back, she realized with dismay that nowhere on Ma's face was there even the slightest suggestion of cosmetics. Suddenly Gwen was very aware of her own bright red lipstick, red nail polish, and dyed blonde curls. Her red silk dress felt entirely inappropriate, and the open-toed shoes, ridiculous.

Gwen's heart sunk. First impressions were so important, and by not understanding this way of life, Gwen felt she had struck out. She looked to her husband for rescuing, still hoping there was a mistake and this pair weren't really his parents.

Then, as disillusioned as she was, she gave her new in-laws a warm smile. Larry smiled as well, and took her arm. The journey to Arborfield had been exhausting, and all Gwen wanted was a cup of tea, a hot bath, and a bed. Everything else could wait until morning.

The group left the train and waited on the platform with their luggage while Pa cranked up the 1925 truck he had borrowed from Larry's boss at the grain elevator. For Gwen, climbing into the truck was no easy feat in her tight dress and high heels, but once she was settled, she snuggled up to Larry, who held his sleeping son against his shoulder.

A few minutes later, they arrived at a cute little bungalow that reminded Gwen of her aunt and uncle's home in England. Looking sentimentally at the bungalow, Gwen smiled to herself and realized that all her fears had come to naught. The house had electricity, a phone, and coal for heat. The stories she had heard from others along her journey about the wilds of Canada, the uncivilized living conditions and strange customs, had been unfounded after all. She only hoped at this point that Ma had bubbles for the bath.

As the group made their way up the walk to the bungalow, Gwen was surprised to see a man and woman standing at the front door. The couple was promptly introduced to Gwen as Larry's boss and his wife. They were very welcoming, and hugged her warmly.

After everyone shed their coats and hats, Gwen and Larry were led to a table laden with all kinds of food. Gwen, now so tired that she felt her head nodding on more than one occasion, could only pick at the food on her plate. The only thing keeping her awake were the countless questions everyone kept asking about her home in England. But to her frustration, whenever she answered their questions, they simply stared blankly at her and asked her to repeat her answer. Gwen wanted to cry. Larry, who had no trouble understanding her despite her accent, had to act as translator. As he spoke, Gwen couldn't help but wonder if the others were simply being obstinate.

Completely exhausted, and not wanting to be rude to her new family and their friends, she leaned over and quietly asked Larry where their bedroom was, as she simply couldn't keep her eyes open a moment longer. Still longing for her bubble bath, she realized she was too tired to make the effort and decided to have one first thing in the morning instead.

Larry smiled and told her they were not at his parents' house; they were at his boss's. His parents' farm was about six kilometres out of town. Then he assured her they wouldn't be staying much longer, as Pa had already gone out to hook the team up to the sleigh.

Gwen looked at him and wondered why he had said sleigh, but decided not to ask. Outside in the cold air, Gwen looked up at the stars above her. She wondered if her aunt and uncle could see what she saw, and then realized it was daytime in England. Biting her lip to stop the tears, she suddenly felt very alone.

The group climbed into the sleigh and then piled blankets on top of themselves. The horses stomped their feet on the frozen turf, impatient for their own barn and bucket of feed. Gwen could smell the animals' sweat, and the acrid odour of fresh manure. Snuggling down in the warmth of the blankets, she decided it wasn't an unpleasant smell after all. In fact, if she wasn't so tired, she suspected the sleigh ride would have been a wonderful experience. But despite her best efforts to stay awake for the ride, her eyelids fluttered closed and she slept all the way out to the farm.

As they approached their destination, Larry nudged Gwen awake. The snow was glowing brightly in the moonlight, and as Gwen struggled to get her bearings, the sleigh pulled to a stop in front of the farmhouse. It was a humble looking building, lonely and forlorn against the white expanse of prairie. The house's siding was unpainted, and bits of tarpaper stuck out randomly here and there. All the stories and warnings Gwen had heard about Canada flooded her tired memory as she untangled her legs from the blankets. Even in the softening light of the moon, the scarred exterior of the farmhouse stared at her apologetically. Gwen sighed.

Entering the only door to the house, the group removed their coats, slipped off their boots, and placed them neatly against the wall. Passing an icebox on the way into the kitchen, Gwen noted the faded and cracked linoleum floor. The kitchen was like no other she had ever seen. It was large and cosy, kept warm by the wood stove that was roaring and crackling in the corner. Wood was stacked neatly against an outside wall, and lying next to the stove on a tattered homemade quilt was a small piglet. The animal was obviously very young and in need of nurturing. A young girl in her mid teens — one of Larry's sisters, Gwen guessed — was at the stove warming milk for the piglet's next feeding. The girl was introduced as Reenie, and she looked shyly over at Gwen and blushed. Gwen smiled uncertainly and then continued to look around.

In the centre of the kitchen was a wooden table with an old-fashioned oilcloth covering the top. The table, surrounded by many wooden chairs, was large enough to seat at least a dozen people. Standing against one wall was a cabinet with a sink for washing vegetables. However, there was no running water. On the floor next to the cabinet was a bucket for slops, and lining three of the walls were shelves stocked with jars of preserves and boxes of Knox Gelatine, Baker's Chocolate, and Magic Baking Powder. Under the shelves were pots, pans, and mugs hanging on hooks. As her eyes scanned the room, Gwen felt as if she had just stepped back in time. Even as tired as she was, her situation hit her hard. Here there would be no luxuries, and lots of hard work.

The group sat down at the large kitchen table, and Ma took Mark with a smile. She told Gwen she'd look after him for the night so that Gwen and Larry could have a good sleep. Gwen wanted to protest, but realized she needed the rest. Besides, Ma had to be capable of babysitting; she'd raised six children.

Larry's youngest sister set out dishes for refreshments. The dishes were plain, old, and functional, and Gwen tried not to compare them to her aunt's fine china. Once again, her eyes welled up with tears as she thought of her family back home. Then, struggling to smile, she told Ma a cup of tea would be lovely.

Ma snorted and said they didn't drink tea, what Gwen needed was a good mug of boiled coffee. A mug was placed in front of her and filled with very strong black coffee. Larry handed her a jug of cream, and told her it was fresh from the cow. Reenie then innocently asked if Gwen had a cow in England.

"Oh yes, there are cows in England," Gwen replied. "But our milk is delivered to our door in glass bottles, by a man in a truck."

Ma and Pa looked at her, and then at each other.

"So's youze never milked a cow?" Ma asked.

"No," she answered.

"Well," Ma said, "we deliver our own milk from the cow's teat to our table. I'll teach youze to milk in a day or two, after you're settled. Nothin' to it, you'll catch on. You can help collect eggs in the mornin's if ya like. I was planning on youze helpin' me cook a roast tomorrow, it's from our steer Willy. Larry said you can make somethin' called york's puddin'?" Then Ma looked over at Larry, her face filled with disbelief at the fact he would marry a girl who had never even milked a cow.

"I'd love to help out where I can, Ma," Gwen said, "but I've never used a wood stove before."

Shocked by this piece of information, Ma asked what it was that Gwen *did* do in England.

"All the usual things," Gwen said, looking down at her coffee.

Ma looked hard at this young woman with the red lipstick, dyed hair, and coloured nails, then got up to pour more coffee. But Gwen hadn't even touched hers — she didn't drink coffee.

As she sat at the large kitchen table, Gwen tried to picture herself in the outfit she was wearing under the belly of a cow. She thought of all her dance classes, elocution lessons, and social etiquette. How many times had Auntie made her leave the room and enter it properly with head held high? And how many times had she practised sitting gracefully with her ankles neatly crossed? Should she explain to Ma that she knew how to order just the right cut from the butcher, brew tea perfectly, and make scones that were lighter than a feather?

Gwen felt like crying. Nervously, she looked at everyone staring at her. Out of the need for something to do, she took a big gulp of hot coffee. She then thanked Ma, and asked Larry to show her to their room, explaining to everyone that all she wanted was a bath and to go to bed. Ma snorted and stated that she was not hauling water from the creek at this time of night for a bath. Especially since it wasn't even Saturday.

Larry took Gwen upstairs to one of the bedrooms on the second floor. There were no handrails along the staircase, nor was there carpet on the steps. None of the rooms upstairs had doors; instead, blankets were hung in the doorways. Larry and Gwen's room had a double bed with homemade quilts on it.

In England, and again in Saskatoon, Larry had warned Gwen that things were simpler in his home-town. He had, indeed, told her of milking cows, hunting, fishing, and dirt farming. Gwen had assumed he was exaggerating some of the stories just to pull her leg. But now, standing in the sparse bedroom, she was beginning to realize the stories had been all too accurate.

After undressing and pulling on a nightshirt, Gwen looked out the bedroom window. The stars were bright, and the wind was blowing puffs of loose snow about. Frost was gathering on the outside of the windowpane. Gwen breathed on the glass and then traced her name in the fog.

Sighing, she slid into bed next to her husband and snuggled in under the quilts. Tomorrow she would ask Larry to haul the water so she could take a nice hot bath. It wasn't Saturday, but she needed to feel the comfort of bubbles and hot water. Then, after she was done with her toiletries, she would go to the corner grocer for tea, and show Ma what civilized people drank in England.

With a smile on her face, she drifted off to sleep.

Gwen and Larry had been asleep about an hour when an awful racket started up outside their bedroom window. Car and truck horns were honking, pots were clanging, and people were shouting. Gwen wondered what was going on, but it was too cold in the room for her to go to the window and look out. Upon hearing Ma get up and hush up the racket, Gwen rolled over and promptly fell back to sleep.

The next morning, Ma explained that some of the townsfolk had thought the newlyweds needed a shivaree. It was a Canadian custom, where the new wife was dragged out of bed in the middle of the night and forced to cook breakfast for the visitors. This was the woman's chance to show all the neighbours and family what a great wife she was, and how lucky her new husband was to marry her.

Ma, realizing Gwen would be lost in the kitchen with that mob watching, sent them all packing. She didn't want the town to know her Larry had brought home an English girl who couldn't cook or milk a cow, and who wanted to take a bath on a Wednesday in the middle of the night. Ma wondered to herself what other surprises this girl had in store for them.

Chapter 4
Life on the Farm

Her first morning on the farm, Gwen woke to a bright and sunny day. The crispness of the air was apparent in the bedroom she shared with her husband. Rolling over in bed, Gwen suddenly realized that Larry was no longer lying beside her. As she listened to the house creak quietly in the stillness, she vaguely wondered if everyone else was still asleep.

Wrapping herself in a quilt, she got out of bed and looked out the window. She was startled at how flat the landscape was, how huge the sky looked, and how far she could see. Peering off into the distance, she could find no indication that Larry's parents had any neighbours.

Gwen dressed quickly while keeping the quilt as snugly around her as possible. She was focused on one thing: a hot bath. Coming down the stairs, she looked at her surroundings. There hadn't seemed to be a toilet upstairs, so without being too nosey, she poked her head around a couple of corners to locate one on the ground floor. Finally, needing to relieve herself rather urgently, she went into the kitchen to find someone who could point her in the right direction.

Larry and Ma were sitting at the table drinking coffee when she entered. No one else was in sight; the smells of breakfast still lingered in the air, but all evidence of the meal had been removed.

Gwen smiled and said good morning. Ma snorted and asked if she would like coffee since it was almost afternoon. Gwen politely declined. The sun was barely up, yet Ma was treating her like she had overslept. Trying not to feel guilty or indignant, Gwen asked Larry to point her in the direction of the toilet. She explained she wanted to freshen up, use the toilet, and have a nice hot bath to start the day.

As Ma stared at Gwen over her mug, a strange grin crept over the older woman's face. Larry smiled and explained the toilet wasn't in the house, but down the hill in a separate building. Ma chuckled and took a sip of her coffee.

Ignoring the chuckle, Gwen gathered her cosmetics and other toiletries then walked down the snowy hill in the direction Larry had indicated. She thought it odd that the toilet would be so far away. However, many things in Canada were strange to her — perhaps all Canadian farms had bathhouses away from the main house.

Suddenly, Gwen stopped dead in her tracks. Before her, standing pitifully in the snow and well lit by the morning sun, was a small wooden outhouse, not a bath-house. She was stunned. The structure was so old that the timbers had shrunk, and she could see inside through the cracks in the walls. Despite the brightness of the morning, the wind was blowing bitterly, and Gwen shivered as she listened to the high-pitched sound of the stiff breeze whistling through the knot-holes. Walking around the offensive building, her disgust deepened when she saw it didn't have a door — the hole of contemplation was exposed for the whole world to see.

Gwen realized she couldn't wait much longer to relieve herself. Groaning in resignation, she stepped into the outhouse, exposed what was necessary, and whistled loudly so she wouldn't be disturbed if anyone came down the path. Her English posterior was soon covered in goose bumps, and the breeze was so cold it froze moisture on contact. Though Gwen's outer self was chilled to the bone, inside she fumed as she recalled the grin on Larry's face when he had given her directions. Her husband was in for it!

From the outhouse's throne — which was nothing more than a hole in a rough wood plank that had been worn smooth by more bottoms than Gwen wanted to consider — was the pretty view of an overgrown duck pond. The trees in the woods beyond were bare of their leaves, and the snow, still piled high, had started to melt, leaving smudges of muck contrasting with the whiteness. In places, long bunches of grass were sticking up through the drifts.

Gwen had difficulty appreciating the prairie scenery, for as new as it was to behold, the air was just too cold for sitting around and taking in the view. Instead, she did what she needed to do as quickly as possible, all the while whistling nervously and watching for bears.

Finished, and shivering so hard that her teeth rattled, Gwen reached around for the toilet paper. There wasn't any. She looked beside her, behind her, and on the floor. All she could find was a copy of the Timothy Eaton's catalogue, opened to a page that had been half torn out. The realization hit her: not only did she have to suffer the indignity of doing her private business in a facility without a door, she also had to stoop to using printed paper to clean herself up. Her "stiff upper lip" was definitely getting a workout.

In a gesture she felt reflected her thoughts on Canadian farm life so far, Gwen tore out a page from the catalogue's farm equipment section and completed her business. Hopping off the plank, she put herself back together and raced up the path to the house, slapping her backside along the way (it was so cold it had gone numb). Inside the warm house once again, she toasted her rear-end in front of the roaring woodstove while Larry and Ma laughed at her.

Gwen plotted her revenge. That night, she started campaigning for her husband to build a door for the outhouse. He thought she was crazy, but she continued to insist. Eventually, with Ma and Pa laughing at him, he built and installed the door, complete with a crescent moon cutout that let the light in when the toilet was occupied. Gwen thanked him profusely, and felt she had dealt a blow on behalf of the civilized world.

After Gwen had been on the farm for a few days, Ma began to teach her what she needed to know about running a household in northern Saskatchewan. Besides the lack of electricity, the biggest challenge for Gwen was the wood stove. It loomed in the corner of the kitchen, taunting her. Try as she might, she simply could not master cooking with it.

Ma knew exactly when to throw in wood, and how much to add to keep the temperature even for cooking or baking. Gwen, however, would forget to stoke the stove altogether, and it would soon be down to a few coals. Realizing her baking was falling, she'd then pile in the wood, and whatever was in the oven would turn black. Larry would come in from the barn, smell the acrid air, and say it was obvious Gwen had been cooking again.

After a week had passed, Gwen was getting sick of trying to cook with the stove. She was also getting tired of hand-washing dirty laundry in a bowl. Frustrated, she asked Ma when the laundry was due to be picked up and delivered. Well, Ma's face was a picture.

"You're in northern Canada," Ma laughed, "and here we do everything ourselves, youngun', even washing our own soiled clothing."

Gwen, disappointed that she would have to continue to do laundry, asked if she could borrow Ma's washer for her and Larry's clothing and bed linens. Her mother-in-law laughed and said she didn't own a laundry machine.

Ma then ordered Gwen to change her clothes, explaining that she would teach her how to do the laundry. Producing an awful metal tub and a scrubbing board, Ma put the tub on the floor and filled the kettle on the stove with snow. Once the snow was melted and the water was boiling, Ma and Gwen skimmed off the residual black bits from the ground snow, and then poured the water into the tub, on top of the dirty clothing. They used Ma's homemade lye soap and rubbed the laundry by hand on the scrubbing board. Twisting each item of clothing hard, they squeezed out the excess water and threw the laundry into another tub of fresh water for rinsing. After each garment was wrung out once more, it was hung outside on the clothesline.

Gwen's fingers turned red and angry. Her long, polished nails softened in the water and broke off on the scrub board. In England, she and her aunt had always sent the dirty linens out to the laundry, and everything came back cleaned, pressed, folded, and delivered right to the door. Gwen had never even considered the work it took to clean clothes.

Once the clean laundry was dry, it was taken off the clothesline and brought into the kitchen for ironing. Ma heated flat irons on the stove, sprinkled the clothes with water, and then showed Gwen how to slap the irons down, and push and press to remove all the creases. At the end of the day, Gwen found that her perception of dirty clothes had changed quite a bit. In England, she would wear something once and then send it out to be cleaned. But now that she was in Canada, she would wear an item again and again until it warranted the work it took to launder it.

Soon after she arrived at the farm, Gwen wrote a letter home to her aunt and uncle, recounting her Canadian experiences thus far. She wrote about the out-house without the door, and the clouds of mosquitoes that seemed to hang in the air just waiting for an English meal. She also told them about burning her fingers as she learned to iron, and her mother-in-law's reaction when she called Mark's dirty diapers "napkins." In Canada, napkins were used to wipe the face when eat-ing, not for wrapping around a baby's bottom.

Gwen wrote about her first batch of bread, which was solid enough to build a new chimney, and explained how Ma regulated the temperature to bake by simply adding one stick of wood on the fire in the right place at the right time. Finally, Gwen complained that the townspeople and neighbours — and even Larry's family — thought her aloof and stuck up. It seemed no matter how hard she worked, there was always so much more that needed doing, and her new family looked at her efforts as small and nowhere near good enough.

Chapter 5
Gwen, This is Arborfield

On Gwen's first Saturday at the farm, Ma announced that the two of them would be attending a get-together in town that afternoon. Gwen asked if she could stay home, as she was feeling a bit overwhelmed with her new lifestyle. But Ma firmly said no; the invitation had been extended specifically so that people could meet her new daughter-in-law. Reluctantly, Gwen got all dolled up in London style, and off they went.

When they arrived at the small bungalow belonging to Larry's boss, Gwen's spirits rose. The house looked as quaint in the daylight as it had in the dark of night. At least there, she knew she could fit in.

Gwen, This is Arborfield

As Gwen and Ma entered through the front door, the woman of the house greeted them warmly. She didn't seem to think the picture hat Gwen was wearing was overdone, nor did she seem to notice how dirty Gwen's feet were from walking up the muddy path to the door in open-toed pumps.

Gwen was ushered to the living room, where she stopped abruptly at the entryway and turned bright red. The room was packed with at least 50 women, all of them looking at her expectantly. There were so many women that they could not all be seated on couches or chairs — some were sitting on the floor, and others were standing along the walls. Gwen stared at the strangers in shocked silence. Then, to her further embarrassment, she was led to a decorated armchair and told that she was the guest of honour at a wedding/baby shower.

"A what?" Gwen whispered to Ma.

"You'll see," Ma said with a smile.

A huge basket of brightly wrapped gifts was set down in front of her. She looked at it in confusion.

"Open the gifts," Ma said, "then pass them around for everyone to look at."

Bewildered, Gwen did as she was told. One by one, she opened the parcels, tearing back paper which revealed household items as well as things for Mark. Among the many gifts was an oddly shaped wooden comb. When Gwen, cheeks burning, asked what this device was for, she was curtly told that it was a blueberry picker. As the women exchanged looks, Gwen's discomfort grew. She decided not to ask any more questions, and simply thanked them all for their generosity.

While everyone was enjoying refreshments, Gwen privately asked Ma why the women were giving her things. She wanted to know if they thought she and Larry were too poor to look after their own affairs. Ma, starting to lose patience, told her it was a wedding shower, and that these things were wedding gifts. It was a Canadian tradition, and since she was now a Canadian, she needed to understand the customs.

Gwen had never heard of a wedding shower, and she couldn't help but suspect that these women were giving her gifts out of charity. After all, she and Larry had been married two years. It seemed strange that the community would decide to celebrate the wedding after all this time. However, swallowing her pride, she tried to be thankful and gracious.

As the gathering was beginning to disperse, a woman approached Gwen. This woman had been sitting close by during the gift opening, and her stares had made Gwen very uncomfortable. She was large, at least a few inches taller than Gwen, and almost as wide as she was tall. She also had the biggest bosom Gwen had ever seen.

The woman stood in front of Gwen for a moment, assessing her before speaking. "I guess Larry told you about us?" she finally asked. "How we was engaged when he went off to the war?" She came closer, and Gwen took a step backwards, looking towards her mother-in-law for rescuing. But Ma had her back turned, and was chatting with another woman across the room.

"I waited for him, eh?" the woman continued. "Then heard he married some skirt in England. And I waited four years for him too."

With an angry look on her face, the woman stepped closer again, her double-D pendulums swinging inches away from Gwen's face. "And youze being an uppity outsider an all — no offence."

Gwen looked the woman directly in the ample cleavage and said, "Well, I certainly understand now that he married me on the rebound since it's plain for everyone to see that you are twice the woman I'll ever be." She smiled her sweetest smile. Hesitating only a moment, the woman returned the smile, and the tension eased.

"Well thank you," the woman said. "I suppose you're all right even if ya can't cook and things." Then she walked away. Gwen's smile widened; she had survived her first Canadian social gathering.

The next day, Sunday, it was Larry's turn to drag

Gwen out of the house. He told her to get cleaned up so that he could take her to meet the neighbours down the hill. Larry explained that these neighbours were bachelors, and that they had lived alone since their sister had gotten married and moved away.

Gwen put on her high-heeled shoes, an expensive grey suit, a black fur jacket, white gloves, and a black, wide-brimmed felt hat. Her long, bleached hair was carefully brushed and curled with hot irons from the stove, and it fell nicely a few inches past her shoulders. After pinching her cheeks for colour, she added a touch of red lipstick and felt sure that this time, she would not embarrass her husband.

Larry, waiting patiently by the truck, smiled a wickedly handsome smile when his wife approached the vehicle. He helped her inside, and was still grinning when they left the farmyard. Gwen asked him if everything was all right.

"Of course," he answered, chuckling. "What could possibly be wrong?"

Moments later, they arrived at the neighbours' property. Gwen knew she was overdressed as soon as she saw the tiny tarpaper shack in the overgrown farmyard. Still, she told herself, she was English, and Larry had said these brothers were from the Netherlands originally — surely they would be civilized enough to appreciate a well-dressed woman.

Larry knocked on the door to the shack, and a gruff voice yelled for them to enter. As the door swung open, Gwen stood on the front stoop and gawked at the three men lounging around a roughly built wooden table. To her surprise and embarrassment, each of them was in various stages of undress. The men were obviously surprised to see Gwen, and they stared openly at the well turned-out woman at their door.

Finally, one of the brothers, the one wearing long-johns and trousers held up by suspenders, pushed a chicken off one of the wooden chairs and offered the seat to Gwen. The second brother, clad only in long-john bottoms with the "trapdoor" slightly askew, ran down to the well to draw water in order to boil fresh coffee. The third brother never moved from the table. He was wearing nothing on his top half, and though she could not see his bottom half, Gwen was almost certain he was naked from the waist down, too. He looked at her and blushed, and she looked at him and blushed.

Gwen kept her eyes averted after that. She drank her coffee, grateful for something to keep her occupied, while Larry chuckled and talked farm talk with the two brothers who were wearing clothes. At the end of the visit, the two brothers walked her and Larry out to the truck, while the third, still blushing profusely, sat firmly in his chair.

The next day, Gwen was once again faced with the task of mastering the kitchen. Ma could bake 16 loaves of bread at a time. Each loaf was fluffy and perfect, and after having lived through years of war rationing, the smell of the baking bread nearly drove Gwen mad. She felt like she was in heaven's kitchen, even though the stove came from Hades.

Indeed, the wood stove was not Gwen's friend. She would forget to stoke it, and dinner would be half raw, or she stoked it too much and everything would be burned. All the cooking skills she had learned back in England were suddenly useless. Humbled, Gwen wondered what Ma must have thought of her, a grown woman who didn't know how to do laundry or iron, and who couldn't even cook.

To make matters worse, Gwen was fairly certain that Ma didn't believe any of her stories about England. Whenever Gwen spoke of her aunt's bone china that was as thin as eggshells, the central heating in the little bungalow at Golders Green, or the milk that was delivered in glass bottles, Ma just looked at her in amazement. Ma also laughed at Gwen's accent, and said that she hoped Mark would learn to talk properly.

Of course, Ma and the wood stove weren't the only challenges for Gwen. It seemed that in Canada, almost everything had a different name: ladders in her stockings were called "runs," and the green grocer was called a "mercantile." Often, Gwen was afraid to open her mouth when she was in the presence of townspeople. If she called the truck a motor car, she was uppity. If she referred to sausages and mashed potatoes as bangers and mash, she was being silly.

Luckily Mark, being so young, fared better. As the first Cramer grandson, his grandparents spoiled him to distraction. Ma and Pa tried to treat Gwen as a daughter, but her strange ways continually made her an outsider. Mark, however, was their son's child, and therefore he had an immediate place of honour in the family.

Not only did Gwen have to do her best to win the hearts of her in-laws, she also had to conquer her fear of wild animals. She didn't like berry picking because of the threat of bears. Even the gophers, as cute as they were, made her nervous with their scurrying about. There was one animal, however, that managed to intrigue her — at least momentarily.

Larry first told her about this mysterious creature when they went for a walk in the woods one afternoon. As they strolled along, Gwen worried about the bears, but Larry told her that he knew for sure there were no bears in the area. Gwen looked at him in disbelief and asked how could he know that. Smiling, Larry said it was because treesqueaks didn't like bears, and if there was a bear in the area, the treesqueaks would hide.

"Treesqueaks?" Gwen questioned.

"Gwen," he said, "didn't I ever tell you about treesqueaks? They're my favourite animals. They're soft like rabbits, with big brown eyes like a deer, and they sit in the trees high above the ground calling to each other. Listen." He stopped talking and waited.

Sure enough, up high and slightly to the left, Gwen heard a creaking sound coming from one of the trees.

"There," said Larry, "did you hear the treesqueak?"

"Yes," smiled Gwen, looking up into the trees to catch a glimpse of the creature. "I want to see one Larry."

When the story of the treesqueaks was relayed to the family at the dinner table that night, Pa laughed so hard that tears fell from his eyes. Ma looked at Gwen in bewilderment, and then chuckled. Larry roared. Gwen, red in the face and recognizing how gullible she had been, tried to take the teasing in good faith, but she silently swore to pay her husband back.

Realizing how embarrassed Gwen was, Ma asked her to tell them how she and Larry met, as they had never heard the story.

"Well," said Gwen, relaxing after the teasing, "we met at a club, and since I worked at the air ministry I knew he pulled a good screw so I told him he could knock me up at eight."

Suddenly, the only sound in the kitchen was Larry choking on his coffee. Ma and Pa stared at Gwen with open mouths. Confused, she could do nothing but stare back at them. After a moment had passed, Pa got up from the table.

"No need for that kind of talk," he said, leaving the house.

Ma followed suit, leaving her son and daughter-in-law alone in the kitchen. Gwen then looked imploringly at Larry, trying to understand what she had done wrong.

Later that evening, Larry tried to explain to his parents that in England, the terms "screw" and "knocking up" had very different meanings than they had in Canada. But even though Ma smiled and nodded politely after the explanation, Gwen knew that her mother-in-law didn't buy a word of it.

Chapter 6
Town Life

fter spending a month on the Cramers' farm, Larry, Gwen, and Mark were finally moving into a home of their own in town.

Town! Gwen could hardly contain her excitement. Even if Arborfield was made up of nothing more than a group of houses, one rickety wooden sidewalk, a beer parlour that only permitted men, and a couple of stores, at least it *sounded* civilized. Besides, they were moving into their own house. No more wood stove, no more coal oil lamps, and no more outhouse.

Or so she thought. On first inspection, Gwen discovered that the house did not have an indoor toilet, but instead boasted the inevitable outhouse in the big back-yard. This wasn't the only disappointment. The sink in the kitchen had plumbing, but only a cold-water pump. When the family needed hot water, Gwen had to use the stove — the wood stove — that stood in the corner of the kitchen. Of course, she often forgot to stoke up the fire; there were plenty of cold washes in the first weeks on their own, to say nothing of half-cooked meals and bread that came out like buckshot.

Larry and Gwen, with all of these challenges, were still very happy to be off the farm. Shortly after they moved, Gwen found out she was pregnant with their second child. Cheerfully, she busied herself with fixing up the house for the new arrival. The nursery required wallpaper, and one day, when Larry was at work, Gwen took Mark down to the hardware store to pick up what she needed. While she was there, she also bought some paint and a few other things to make the redecorating easier.

After paying for her purchases, she realized she would not be able to carry everything home with a toddler in tow. Fortunately, there was a man near the counter who seemed to be an employee. He looked a little old to be an errand boy, but Gwen thought it was wonderful that the shop owner would give this small, elderly man a job. The man kindly offered to carry the items home for Gwen. She gratefully accepted, happy that there was at least one shop in town that did business the same way the English did.

By the time they reached the house, Gwen was feeling quite sorry for the older man. The items were heavy, and he was skinny. In fact, it looked like he could have really used a good meal. She opened the front door of the house for him, and he thoughtfully put the items in the room where they would be used. Gwen reached in her purse for a tip, and felt terrible when she discovered she only had a quarter. Apologetically, she handed over the coin and thanked him "ever so much." The little man chuckled and thanked her, putting the quarter in his shirt pocket. As he made his way down the front walk, he looked back at the house and chuckled again.

When Larry arrived home from work, Gwen told him the story, and asked if he would give the man something extra the next time they were in the hardware store. Larry laughed and said like heck he would, the little man was the town's millionaire. Not only did he own a couple of sections of land outside Arborfield, he also owned the hardware store, several houses, and a garage.

Gwen figured it would be a long time before she would live that one down — and she was right. Soon the story of the crazy English girl tipping the town millionaire a quarter was being spread around the community.

Town Life

After having settled into the new home, Gwen decided it was time to invite Larry's boss and the boss's wife over for dinner. Gwen vowed to herself that she'd show them all what a great cook she was by serving them a traditional English meal. She rose early to begin work on the meal, preparing the roast beef by searing it on the outside in hot butter and spicing it the way her aunt had taught her. She peeled carrots and blanched potatoes, and placed them around the roast, along with onions and celery. Then, humming happily to herself, she put the roast in the oven and turned her attention to dessert.

It was a hot day in August, and Gwen decided that fresh peaches served with English-style clotted cream would be a refreshing dessert. She washed, sliced, and pitted the peaches, putting the clotted cream on them before placing them in the icebox to keep cool until dinner. Then she cracked several eggs, whipped them by hand until they were frothy, and put them in the icebox until they were needed for the Yorkshire pudding.

Setting the table, Gwen was careful to put the butter in a dish of ice so that it wouldn't melt in the heat. She also made aspic jelly, and placed it on the table alongside the butter.

Pleased with everything, she washed, changed, and waited for her company. They arrived right on schedule, and Larry served them pre-dinner drinks in the front room.

After a polite period of time had passed, Gwen excused herself to take the roast out of the oven and start on the Yorkshire pudding and gravy. As she opened the wood stove, her heart hit her feet. She had forgotten to stoke the stove and it was completely out. The roast was red and barely cooked, the carrots were still crunchy, and the oven was nowhere near hot enough for cooking the Yorkshire pudding. Gwen told Larry to stall the company with another drink while she handled the emergency.

Unfortunately, while she was struggling in the kitchen, the ice around the butter melted, overflowed the dish, and soaked the tablecloth. The aspic jelly was also beginning to melt, and it leaned precariously to one side, threatening to land on the table.

Gwen carved the roast as best she could, slicing off the parts that looked cooked. She called everyone to the table, and her company sat down just as the aspic jelly got tired of leaning. The roast was so rare it almost jumped off the serving dish, and Gwen was so distraught that she was ready to cry.

Larry made some jokes, poured her a large glass of sherry, and soon she was feeling better. She figured at least the dessert would be fine; the peaches didn't need to be cooked, and they certainly wouldn't melt in the heat.

But as it turned out, the peaches weren't at all ripe; they were hard and sour. Gwen almost cried again when she brought them out to the table. To make matters worse, the cream had curdled, and even sugar couldn't sweeten the fruit up enough to make it edible.

Despite all of this, the company was very gracious, and as far as Gwen knew, they never told a soul about the dinner — if they had, it would have been all over town in no time flat. But what Gwen didn't realize was that the couple had no idea the dinner was a failure; they simply thought the English had peculiar taste in food.

Not long after the disappointing dinner party, Ma asked Gwen to accompany her on a visit to a farm deep in the bush. The family that lived on the farm was poor, and the woman had several children. Ma warned Gwen that the woman was not careful about her appearance, so not to expect too much. Gwen simply laughed in response.

When they arrived at the farm, Gwen was stunned. Surrounding a very dilapidated house was the most beautiful garden she had ever seen. It seemed the woman was able to grow anything.

However, upon entering the farmhouse, Gwen

quickly realized the woman's talents didn't extend much beyond gardening. Her house — if you could call it that — was nothing more than an old, unpainted shack with a homemade board table and some benches inside.

The woman had been baking that day, and there was bread rising on the counter. But because there were no screens on the door or windows, the bread was covered with flies. As the women had tea and chatted, ducks waddled in and out of the house at will. Then, in the middle of the conversation, the woman plopped her two-year-old on her lap, lifted her top and, while farm hands and her husband came in and out of the kitchen, let the child suck noisily. Gwen, coming from a country where bottles were the normal method of feeding children, was most embarrassed, and tried to look everywhere but at the woman. Ma just smiled widely, and chuckled.

During the course of the visit, the woman's husband, who seemed clean and nice enough, brought in the family goat. Gwen's mouth dropped as he stood the goat on the table where they were sitting, and milked it. She was speechless. Ma, deciding that her daughter-in-law had had enough of a culture shock for one day, said it was time for them to be on their way home.

After visiting the farm and seeing the woman's wonderful garden, Gwen was inspired to try her own hand at growing things. She went to the hardware store and read the seed packages for sale, picking out a package she felt she could handle without too much difficulty.

Bringing home the seeds and following the directions closely, she set out the area and asked Larry to help her get it ready for planting. Larry broke the sod and hoed the area free of weeds and rocks, then Gwen shooed him away. She truly felt she had something to prove: English or not, she could grow a garden just like anyone else.

When Larry was at work, she reread the planting directions carefully. She was to put the seeds in hills and cover them with dirt. It didn't say anywhere how high to make the hills, so she formed a couple of rows about a foot apart with hills about a foot high. On the top of each hill, she carefully placed one seed and covered it over with a bit of dirt, then watered it. Daily, she went out to look at each hill for the first sign of new growth. Within a few days there was a small sprout of green and Gwen was thrilled. She began to tell the neighbours about her garden.

One neighbour came over to look, and smiled widely as she praised the garden. Apparently, the woman commented to Ma about it in town one day, and asked Ma if she knew what the funny English girl thought she was growing. So Ma, curious, decided to pay her daughter-in-law a visit. When Gwen showed her the backyard, Ma burst out laughing. Only one hill sprouted a single vine. On that vine was a single pickling cucumber. Gwen was very hurt, she was quite proud of that cucumber.

When summer arrived, Gwen and Mark picked all kinds of berries that grew fairly close to town. Gwen refused to take Mark too far away, sure that they would stumble upon a bear. With Ma's help, she canned much of the fruit they picked, and made pies and cobblers out of the rest. By the end of the summer, she had canned 90 litres of saskatoons and several litres of blueberries. Larry was very impressed with how quickly Gwen was adapting to prairie life.

One day, Larry brought home a case of crab apples and told Gwen not to tackle them until he returned from work the following day, as she had never canned crab apples before. Gwen, however, ignored his request. She decided to can the crab apples while Larry was away at work so that she could surprise him with a dish of them for dessert after dinner that night.

Gwen hunted through her recipe book and found directions for canning crab apples. Cleaning them all, she stoked up the woodstove, and by the end of the day she had the whole case put up.

Larry was very impressed when he got home from

work and saw 26 jars of fruit sitting on the kitchen counter. After dinner, he waited eagerly for Gwen to dish up dessert, as crab apples were his favourite. Pouring a liberal amount of cream over the plump fruit, he thought it a bit odd when the cream appeared to be curdling, but he dug in with gusto anyway. Almost immediately, he choked and sputtered. Gwen hadn't canned the crab apples in syrup; she had pickled them in vinegar.

Chapter 7
Trapping

Pa was quite a trapper, and ran lines all winter. Every week, weather permitting, he made the long trek into the wilderness to check his lines. He was mostly after ermine, beaver, and rabbit furs. Larry often accompanied his Pa, taking his rifle along so that he could supplement the larder with whatever game he could shoot. Gwen enjoyed rabbit, as long as she didn't know what it was ahead of time. Venison was also okay, but it had to be cooked right. Ma's venison was wonderful, but Gwen's had a long way to go.

One November afternoon, Larry told Gwen that he thought she needed a change of pace. He offered to look after Mark so that she could go with Pa to check the traplines. She was thrilled, wanting to learn as much about her new country as she could. She also felt that since she wore fur, she should see first-hand how it was acquired.

After loading the sleigh, Larry bundled up Mark and drove his small family over to the parents' farm. He planned to visit with Ma while Gwen and Pa were off trekking. The lines Pa was checking that day were close to home, they were mostly along the creek and the duck pond, and a few were set along a rabbit trail in the woods.

It was a crisp, clear day, and as Gwen and Pa breathed, clouds of white puffed out of their mouths. Though the temperature was cold, Gwen loved bright, winter days on the prairie. It seemed as though she could see forever; the land was so flat, the sky so huge, and the white of the snow made everything look clean. Gwen swore that it was so flat in northern Saskatchewan that if a person's dog ran away from home, three days later that person could stand on his or her porch and still see it running.

Gwen had to struggle to keep up with Pa, and she watched the woods constantly for bears. Pa laughed at his daughter-in-law; everyone knew bears hibernated in the winter, but Gwen was fixated on the creatures. Every picnic, walk in the woods, or trip to the outhouse was an ordeal for her. Every time she saw a dark shape in the distance, spotted tracks in the snow, or heard a noise outside at night, she was sure a bear was lurking nearby. It made no difference that Larry and his parents assured her that bears hadn't been sighted in the area for years. She simply didn't believe it.

The first trapline in the woods proved productive. Three snow-white rabbits had been caught in the snare. They looked twisted in death, as if they had fought valiantly near the end. Though Gwen felt a twinge of sympathy for the rabbits, she realized that the snare would have killed them quickly, and was satisfied the animals had barely suffered at all.

Pa kept Gwen at a distance and off the rabbit trail so that her scent wouldn't come close to the line. Careful to touch only what was necessary, he freed the frozen carcasses from the snare. He explained he had to replace the snare's old wire with a new one that didn't smell of death, so other animals would continue using the path. Then he carefully took a rabbit skin out of his pack and laid it on some fresh snow. Unwrapping it, Pa revealed a pair of mitts. Without touching the outside of the mitts, he slipped his hands in them and reset the lines.

Pa explained that the mitts had been left outside on the line for a week so that the smell of human would be faint or erased altogether by the wind and cold temperatures. Then they were carefully wrapped in a fresh rabbit skin and put in his pack so that the rabbits and other animals wouldn't find the odour offensive. Gwen was fascinated, and realized that this man — who was lacking many social graces and would undoubtedly appal her Aunt Ivy with his demeanour and manners — was educated and intelligent in ways she could only imagine. She suddenly recognized that out there in the woods, how you sipped your tea really wasn't important.

As Pa worked, he talked. He was usually so quiet on the farm, and Gwen enjoyed discovering this new side of her father-in-law. He told her of the early Native tribes that once roamed over this land, and of all the Native artifacts that he'd found on the homestead when he first broke sod in 1914. He had discovered ancient hunting camps, as well as arrowheads, stone blades, and hammers of smoothed rock.

Pa told Gwen that he admired the Native way of life. Early Native peoples were so in tune with the world around them that when they made a kill, they prayed over the dead animal and asked its spirit to forgive them. Believing waste was against the gods of the earth, sky, and sun, they used every part of the animal. Ma and Pa both hated waste. They spent much of their time using and reusing items.

The next trapline Pa decided to check was the one at the beaver pond. He had placed traps over the bank where the beavers came ashore to harvest their birch trees and drag them into the water.

As Pa hauled the first trap out of the water and onto the bank, Gwen saw that it had a fresh catch. A young beaver, crying like a baby, was caught by one front leg. The animal's little moans and whimpers sounded human, and when Pa hit it over the back of the head with the blunt end of his hatchet, it raised its one good paw as if to ward off the blow. The sound was like that of an egg breaking.

Gwen felt ill as she watched Pa clean the still-warm animal. He explained that the frozen carcasses could be taken home and thawed before skinning, but that he preferred skinning the warm ones on the trail, especially beaver, since the family didn't eat beaver meat.

While Pa skinned the animal, Gwen turned her back and closed her eyes. Her mind kept replaying the sound of the beaver's cries and the skull cracking that put the poor creature out of its misery. She decided she couldn't stomach seeing any more, and asked Pa if she could go back to the farm. Surprised, but trying to be understanding, he pointed her in the direction of the path home. She wasn't far, and Pa promised that when he finished at the pond he would follow to make sure she arrived safely.

That evening, when Gwen got home, she threw away all the fur she had brought from England, all the hats and ornamental collars. After seeing the beaver's suffering, the items no longer seemed fashionable. All she could see when she looked at them was death. From then on, she swore that she would only wear fur for warmth. If animals had to die for her, then she would make sure that her clothing reflected their sacrifice and not her selfish vanity.

The day's outing had also increased her respect for her father-in-law and all he did. He worked hard for his family, and did so without complaint. When Pa heard about Gwen's reaction to her excursion, he chuckled and shook his head. "The English have strange ways," he said.

Just weeks after Gwen went with Pa to check his traplines, she gave birth to her second child. Larry and Gwen's daughter, Wendy, was born in the local nursing home. She was a pretty little thing, with big eyes, and lots of dark hair.

Chapter 8
Back to the Farm

Gwen and Larry had been living in town for two years when Larry and his brother Murray decided to go into a farming partnership. Purchasing an old farm outside of Arborfield, the brothers began making their plans to grow grain.

The winter before the family was to leave their home in Arborfield to move out to the farm, Gwen decided she would put her dance training to good use. To earn some extra cash for Christmas, she started a dance school. Soon, she had about 15 pupils, and another English war bride assisted her.

The two planned a Christmas concert. Gwen wanted

some money to buy Mark a tricycle and Wendy a big doll. She and Larry were also trying to save for the move, and the extra cash from the ticket sales would certainly help them.

The night of the concert was cold but bright. Larry was the master of ceremonies for the evening. He had taken on extra work to earn money for some badly needed farm equipment. In addition to his grain elevator job, he was working part-time helping the local electricians fill and deliver all the Christmas orders. He was very tired, and fortified himself with a bottle of coke that had a shot of rum in it.

Someone also laced the children's punch with moonshine, and as the evening wore on, Larry's jokes became funnier and the crowd became noisier. Gwen was mortified when she discovered that everyone at the concert was getting drunk on the punch. She enlisted some help, made fresh, alcohol-free drinks, and the concert went on. All in all, the show was a hit; the kids were adorable, the parents were proud, and Gwen was pleased with the turnout.

After the concert, there was a dance to top off the evening. By the end of the event, Gwen had made enough money to pay for the refreshments, the hall rental, and the band. She also had a tidy sum left over to put towards the upcoming move and buy a few Christmas presents.

A photograph of Gwen and Larry
taken around the time they left Arborfield.

The children had a good Christmas. Mark loved his bike and wouldn't go to sleep at night without parking it at the end of his bed. Wendy loved her doll, but she liked her brother's bike better.

Back to the Farm

When spring came after another long winter, Gwen and Larry packed up their house, said goodbye to their neighbours of two years, and moved to the farm. The property was only a few kilometres from Ma and Pa's homestead.

The farmhouse was a draughty old wreck of a place, but Gwen worked hard to make it as cosy as possible. The heater was more than 20 centimetres off the ground, and the loose windows and cracks under the doorways kept the floors cold. Gwen worried that her family would all freeze when winter arrived. But Ma, ever practical, gave her some rags and showed her how to make braided rugs for the floor.

After that, nothing in the house was safe. Any article of clothing Gwen could get her hands on was ripped into strips and braided. She also sewed tubes of cloth, stuffed them with scrap material, and laid them along window ledges and doors to try to keep out some of the cold air.

Ma and Pa owned an old Durant car. Since Larry and Gwen now had two children, their truck wasn't appropriate for transporting the whole family for long distances. So, for the occasional outing, they borrowed the Durant, which ran fine except for the fact it continually ran out of water.

One sunny summer day, after the family had settled into the farmhouse, Larry and Gwen decided to take the children out for a ride in the country. They packed a picnic, and some extra water for the Durant, and went to find a place where the children could play and explore.

It had been a particularly hot summer, and most of the watering holes and creeks had long since dried up. Except for a few muddy spots in the bottoms of the creek beds, there wasn't any ground water to be found.

On the way home, the car overheated and needed more water. All the water they packed had been used, and the ditches were dry. Since they were still too far to attempt walking home, Gwen suggested that Larry try to find a farm somewhere nearby. Larry nodded in agreement and promised to be back soon. A few minutes later, he emerged from the bush holding a rusty can filled with water. Smiling, he poured it into the car's radiator, and off then went.

As they drove, Gwen marvelled at how fortunate it was that Larry had found a farm so close by. Larry chuckled and said he didn't get the water from a farm.

"A creek then?" she asked.

"No." he answered, "it was left over from the juice I drank at lunch."

Gwen was disgusted, and Larry laughed all the way to the nearest riverbank, where they filled up with fresh water for the trip home.

That fall, right after the harvest, the farmers in the area held their annual jamboree at the curling rink in town. Every year, the party included games, raffles, and a dance with refreshments. The band was made up of local musicians, and occasionally Pa played the fiddle or called the square dances.This year, however, Ma and Pa decided not to attend. Instead, they offered to look after Mark and Wendy so that Gwen could go to her first prairie jamboree.

Excited, Larry took Gwen into Tisdale, about 60 kilometres away, to buy new clothes for the occasion. On the night of the dance, they dolled themselves up. Larry had even purchased a new pair of shoes.

The children were dropped off at their grandparents' house, and Gwen and Larry made their way to the dance. When they arrived at the curling rink, Larry parked the truck in front of the building and told his wife he needed to run over to the store to buy some cigarettes. Gwen nodded, got out of the truck, and waited for Larry in the entrance to the hall, listening to the music.

She waited a long time. Every now and again, she'd go outside to see if she could see him coming, but no such luck. He was gone so long she thought something must were happened to him and she began to worry. Pacing between the rink and the truck, she looked up and down the street, growing more and more anxious as time went on.

When Larry had left Gwen at the truck, he'd decided to take a shortcut to the store by cutting across someone's backyard. Little did he know that the people who owned the property had just recently dug a new hole for their outhouse. Earlier that day, they had dragged their outhouse off the old hole, and planned to fill it in the following morning.

In the dark, Larry had missed seeing the old sewage-filled hole, and he fell in all the way up to his chest. It took him at least half an hour to pull himself out, gagging and vomiting the whole time. He arrived at the curling rink plastered with sewage, and weak and sick from the smell. Gwen stared at her husband in shock. The stench was unbelievable, and while she was concerned about his well-being, she couldn't get near him for the smell.

Larry climbed into the truck and opened the window; Gwen got into the passenger's side and opened her window as well. They drove home with Larry hanging his head out one side for air, and Gwen hanging her head out the other. Of course, between gasps, Larry was cursing and gagging, and Gwen was laughing and gagging.

There was a bright harvest moon shining that night, and Gwen made Larry stand outside in the farmyard and strip off his clothes. She brought him the metal tub and some of Ma's homemade lye soap. The stove was out, so Larry, standing naked in the moonlight, had to scrub himself with cold water from the pump. He shivered, gagged, and shivered some more. Finally, he was clean enough, and he came inside covered in a blanket. He looked so pathetic that Gwen burst out laughing all over again.

The next day, Larry buried his new suit and shoes, and he and Gwen went to pick the kids up from their grandparents' house. Ma and Pa chuckled hard when they heard the story of the night's escapades. Gwen told them Larry looked like a Rodin statue, all white in the moonlight. Larry glared at her, and they all laughed. Gwen was pleased — it was the first time since she'd arrived from England that they were laughing at some-thing someone else had done. She began to feel like part of the family.

It was a week before Larry could stomach eating.

On New Years Eve, Ma offered to mind the children so that Gwen and Larry could try to attend another local dance. This time, Larry avoided taking any shortcuts, and the couple had a good time at the party. However, as soon as the New Year came in, they decided to hurry home, as a bad snowstorm was on its way. Larry, trying to get to there as quickly as possible, swerved too

sharply around a bend and hit a snowdrift about a kilometre from the farm. The couple had to walk the rest of
the way, and Gwen, wearing dancing shoes, was chilled
to the bone by the time they reached the house. The
next day, Larry retrieved the truck and collected the
children from his parents. That New Year's dance was
Gwen's last venture away from the farm for the next
three months, as storm after storm hit.

One of the first things Larry had done when they
had moved to the farm was run a clothesline from the
house to the barn. This line acted as his guide in the
blizzards so he could find his way to the barn and back
without getting lost. When he told Gwen how a whiteout
could get you lost feet away from your house, Gwen
thought that he was pulling her leg. However, after the
first blizzard hit, she realized his story was not so far-
fetched after all — in fact, it was frighteningly accurate.

The first winter on the farm was a hard one. Gwen
found herself housebound with two small children for
weeks at a time. Her slight frame was no match for the
wind that howled and almost toppled her whenever she
ventured outside. She was always bundled so thorough-
ly against the cold that she was afraid if she ever did fall
down, she wouldn't be able to bend enough to get back
up again.

Larry didn't seem to slow down much that winter.

He went to town once a week for the mail and supplies, same as Pa. He did the chores, looked after the animals in the barn, and helped haul tubs of snow into the house for melting, and wood for the stove in the kitchen. Throughout the winter, Gwen suffered long bouts of homesickness, cried sometimes for days, and barely spoke to others. The brutal weather was a shock to her. She had known there was snow in Canada, but she wasn't prepared for this. The cold was like nothing she had ever experienced, and with every passing day, the house seemed to grow smaller, closing in on her.

Gwen spent many hours pouring over letters from her family back in England. Occasionally, she slammed cupboard doors in frustration, and threw books or dishes. No one, not her in-laws, her new acquaintances in town, or even Larry, could understand her frustrations.

Chapter 9
"Bear! Bear!"

The following spring, Larry and his brother decided to work the farm in two shifts, daytime and nighttime, rotating every two weeks. The first night shift was to be Larry's. The plan was that every evening at dusk, he would head to the fields to plough and prepare for planting, and then come home every morning at dawn.

Gwen quaked at the idea and said, "You can't leave me here all night on my own. I'm too scared. We're miles from anywhere."

Larry laughed and told her to leave the coal oil lamp on and she'd be perfectly safe. To ease her mind a bit, he filled the lamp for her and lit it before he left; she was frightened of the thing. He took the other lamp with him.

The first night passed smoothly, and Gwen and the children slept well. When Larry came home that morning, his wife seemed content and rested, and he thought things would be easy from that point on. Gwen, however, couldn't help but feel a little disappointed that her husband hadn't even acknowledged her achievement. After all, she had managed to spend a whole night on the prairie alone. She knew farm wives were supposed to spend many nights on their own, looking after livestock and children while their husbands were away. But she was from England, and for that reason alone, she felt some recognition of her accomplishment should be noted. Larry, of course, simply laughed when she brought it up later that day. Then he filled and lit the lamp for her and went off to work, just as he had the night before.

Darkness fell, and Gwen trimmed the lamp low. The children drifted off to sleep and Gwen, weary from a hard day's work, went upstairs to turn in as well. But the second she started to drift off, there was a loud bump outside the window, and she heard the children's wagon being knocked around the yard.

Not surprisingly, a bear was the first thought that came to her mind. She was sure the animal had smelled the children and was trying to break into the house. Again she heard a thump, and her heart started to race. Terrified, she spotted the lamp burning on the other side of the room. Thinking she could set the bush outside on fire as a signal for help, and possibly even scare the bear away with the flames, she tossed the lamp out the window with all her might.

Unfortunately, the lamp blew out as it fell from the window, and everything went dark. Gwen heard the sound of metal hitting the ground off somewhere in the distance. There was no fire, and without the lamp, the whole house was shrouded in blackness. Gwen was near hysterics.

Worried about the children's safety, she ventured into the dark hallway and felt along the wall until she reached their room. Waking Mark, she scooped Wendy into her arms and the group felt their way back along the hall to Gwen and Larry's room. Then, venturing out into the hallway again, Gwen pushed all the furniture she could move down the stairs and lodged it against the front door. Dressers, beds, night tables, bedding — everything she could shift or toss, bumped and crashed down the staircase until there was nothing left to throw.

Meanwhile, the thumping and shuffling outside continued. Gwen, fearing the worst, stuck her head out her bedroom window and yelled and screamed as loudly as she could, over and over, hoping that Larry would hear her and come running.

But no one came, and hour after hour ticked by as the animal noises continued in the yard. Gwen lost her voice with all the screaming, and the children lay frightened in the bed, in the dark.

At about 4 a.m. it started to rain, and the rain turned into a downpour. Larry, who had been trying to plough, realized it was too wet to continue, and he packed up to go home early. Arriving home just as the grey was beginning to show on the horizon, he was surprised to find that he couldn't open the front door. There was no light showing from the upstairs window, and no signs of life anywhere in the house. Larry banged on the door and called for his wife to let him in.

Finally, a voiceless Gwen stuck her head out of the upstairs window. She wanted to warn him to watch out for the bear, but her voice came out as a dry whisper and, out of frustration and fear, she started to cry. There was so much furniture on the stairs that she couldn't even get down them to let him in.

Mark came to the window and told his dad that the door was stuck and they couldn't get down the stairs. So Larry wiggled a window open and crawled through. After clearing the furniture from the stairs, he came into the bedroom with a lamp. Gwen was still crying, and

Mark had to explain that there was a bear outside.

Curious, Larry went outside in the new morning light to investigate. He found the lamp about a metre away from the bush. It was empty of oil and a little bent from hitting the ground, but still serviceable. Soon after he found the lamp, Larry found the family cow, chewing her cud after making a meal of the kitchen vegetable patch. Gwen, overtired the night before, had forgotten to lock her in the barn. Daisy, the family Jersey, was the bear.

All the same, Gwen flatly refused to be left alone with the children the following night. After packing up some bedding and other essentials, she informed Larry that if he insisted on working at night, then they would all have to go out to the field together. Larry agreed and told her he would tow the bunkhouse out to the field he was working on. That way, she and the children could sleep nearby, and he could keep on working.

The bunkhouse was used for threshing crews and labourers during the busiest part of the season. Built on skids, it was often towed into the fields for night crews. Larry hooked the bunkhouse to the tractor and towed it, bumping and banging, out to the field. After checking to make sure there were no mice in the stove and pipes, he lit the lamp for Gwen and told her that if she needed anything — or was frightened by another cow — she was to wave the lamp in the window as a signal, and he would come running.

When he left, Gwen warily took in her surroundings. The bunkhouse was a dreary affair, with an old iron bedstead, one tiny, dusty window, and a lone cupboard fastened to the wall. Beneath the cupboard, enamel cups and other appliances dangled precariously on rusting hooks. A large potbellied stove stood in the middle of the room, flanked by two wooden chairs. Gwen sighed. For tonight, this was home, and the kids went right to sleep.

Everything was fine for a while; the bunkhouse was in the centre of the field, and Larry was working in circles around it. However, as the night wore on, his circles were getting bigger and he gradually moved farther and farther away from Gwen and the children. The farther away he was, the more nervous Gwen became.

Dozing fitfully, Gwen jerked awake upon hearing an unfamiliar noise outside. As she listened, she realized that Larry's tractor sounded a long way off. Soon, she was sure she could hear animal noises, and imagined all sorts of predators out for a night's hunting. Limp with fright, she grabbed the lamp and started swinging it frantically in the window, praying Larry would notice it.

He did, and a few minutes later, he buzzed his way over on the tractor and asked what was wrong.

"I saw eyes looking in at us through the window," Gwen explained, stammering.

Larry took his lamp and walked around the outside of the bunkhouse to inspect the soft earth. He laughed. It was only a deer, he told her, and since the deer in Canada preferred grain and grass to skinny English women, she had nothing to fear. Then he shook his head and told her to go to sleep so he could get some work done.

Gwen was furious, and still frightened beyond reason. As the sound of the tractor faded into the night, her panic rose and she waved the lamp in the window again, determined that he would not leave her alone in an old bunkhouse in the middle of a field.

Once again, Larry drove over on the tractor, but this time, he didn't bother to step foot in the bunkhouse. Instead, he hooked the bunkhouse up to the tractor and dragged it around the field while he carried on with his work. Inside, the stove jiggled, the cups banged, the walls creaked, and Gwen fumed. Only the children slept while they were dragged in circles around the field for the rest of the night.

In the morning, Larry's brother came out to the field to take over. When he saw Larry on the tractor, towing the bunkhouse, he started to laugh. Soon, the whole town was talking about the bear, the deer, and Gwen being towed around behind Larry's tractor all night.

The spring was a difficult one for Gwen and Larry. Mark came down with pneumonia and was admitted to the hospital in Tisdale for a week. Wendy was crawling everywhere, and soon was pulling herself up to standing position. With all the canning and preserving Gwen had to do on top of running to and from the hospital, looking after an active baby, and trying to harvest, she had her hands full.

One Saturday, Larry's sister came to help Gwen with the children and the canning. Mark had only been home a couple of days, and Wendy was determined to follow her brother everywhere. As the two children raced around the house, Gwen and her sister-in-law set to work on the canning. Gwen had picked all the beans and chopped them so that they were ready for the jars. On the stove was a tub of boiling water to blanch the vegetables, and another of boiling brine to pour over them in the jars before sealing. Larry's sister had laid the highchair and some kitchen chairs in the doorway to the kitchen to keep the children away from the hot stove.

Struggling with a hot pot of beans, Gwen turned and drained the boiling water into a bucket on the floor, then went over to the sink full of cold water, where she plunged the vegetables before putting them in jars. As she turned from the sink, she saw Wendy. The baby had crawled through the hole in the highchair, pulled herself to a standing position, and was taking a couple of shaky steps across the kitchen floor with her hands extended. Gwen yelled and rushed forward to grab the child, but she was too late. Wendy fell as she reached the bucket of boiling water, knocking it over and dousing herself from head to toe.

Wendy screamed, Gwen screamed, and Larry's sister ran to fetch Larry from the field. Angry blisters were quickly forming on the side of the baby's face, as well as on her arms, stomach, and legs. Gwen placed butter and ice on Wendy's delicate skin, and then wrapped her in a clean, wet sheet to reduce the burning.

Larry charged into the kitchen and scooped up the screaming toddler. Gwen raced on ahead and got into the truck so that Larry could place Wendy on her lap. They drove six kilometres into town, and when they pulled up in front of the doctor's office, their hearts hit the floor. On the door was a note stating the doctor was away fishing. So, all they could do was drive another 60 kilometres to the nearest hospital in Tisdale.

The burns were bad, but fortunately for Wendy, the doctor tried a new drug to see if that would help the healing process. Wendy was given one of the first doses of penicillin to be administered in the area, and was soon well on the road to recovery.

Nevertheless, the episode was the last straw for Larry and Gwen; they decided to pack up and move to Edmonton. Larry would find work in the city, Gwen would have electricity, and the children would have doctors close by.

It wasn't a difficult choice to make, to give up the farm. The crops were poor, and farming was a lot of work with no returns and quite a bit of expense. In the two years they had been on their farm, one crop had rained out, and a clover crop had been blown away by the wind right before the harvest. The family was tired of struggling with farm life, and Gwen finally admitted that try as she might, she would never be a farmer's wife.

With bittersweet goodbyes, the Cramer family packed their things and made for the city of Edmonton. Gwen knew she would miss many things about their life in northern Saskatchewan: Ma, Pa, the community dances. Of course, there were things she wouldn't miss, but would never forget: the outhouse without the door, the treesqueaks, and Ma's majestic wood stove.

Epilogue

The day shone clear and bright. Somewhere in the distance a firecracker exploded. It was October 30, 1988, and people were getting ready for Halloween.

Next to a small Pentecostal church in Chemainus, British Columbia, there was silence in the graveyard. A wind stirred the trees and a maple leaf, brown with touches of gold, drifted slowly to the earth in a spiral of autumn colour. Gwen Cramer stood holding the arm of her eldest son, Mark, as the minister began the last burying rights of her husband, Larry Cramer.

Around Larry's gravesite stood men and women clad in legion uniforms, and around Gwen were her five children, their spouses, and 14 grandchildren. Each child marked the path of the family's travels since Gwen had immigrated to Canada in 1946. Mark, the eldest, was born in England; Wendy in Arborfield, Saskatchewan; Bryan in Edmonton; Cynthia in Calgary; and the youngest child, Della, was born in Red Deer, Alberta. All the grandchildren were born on Vancouver Island, British Columbia, where Larry and Gwen had finally settled in 1966.

They say you can take the boy away from the farm

but you can't take the farm out of the boy. In Larry's case, the saying proved true. In Chemainus the couple had retired on an acre of land, where they cared for a dairy cow, chickens, a fishpond with koi and turtles, and an enormous vegetable garden.

As happy as Larry had been in Chemainus, Gwen had been equally content; not only had she been living close to the ocean, she also had indoor plumbing. At the time of his death, Larry and Gwen Cramer had been married 48 years.

Today, Gwen lives in a highrise in Victoria, British Columbia. Everywhere in her home are pictures of Larry, as well as her family here in Canada and in England. Gwen speaks with an English accent, her hair is coloured, and she never leaves her apartment without looking her best. The receptionist at her doctor's office refers to her as Mrs. Hollywood because she is so well turned-out.

When asked what she would change in her life if she had the chance, Gwen said she wouldn't have agreed to go out to the farm after the war in 1946. She said she was never a farm girl, and while the people were wonderful and the town was cute, she was a lime in an apple barrel.

Between the years 1942 and 1947, the Canadian government transported nearly 48,000 war brides and their 22,000 children to this country. Some war brides couldn't make the transition, and left their husbands to return to their families back home. Gwen said the thought had crossed her mind once in the middle of a blizzard, with crying children and the wind howling through the cracks under the doors. However, even after all these years, she's glad she came, glad she stayed, and is very proud to be a Canadian.

Acknowledgments

This story was the true story of Gwendoline (Haskell) Cramer. The situations depicted in this book were taken with her permission from her journal and memories, and augmented by historical facts.

Photo Credits

All photographs are from Gwendoline Cramer's own collections.

ISBN 1-55153-977-2

About the Author

A mother of three, Cynthia J. Faryon is an international-ly published author and freelance writer residing in Richer, Manitoba. Canadian born, she focuses her writing on Canadian content, covering topics such as travel, family issues, biography, and history. This is Cynthia's second book in the Amazing Stories series.

Amazing Stories™

MARIE-ANNE LAGIMODIÈRE

The Incredible Story of
Louis Riel's Grandmother

HISTORY/BIOGRAPHY

by Irene Ternier Gordon

ISBN 1-55153-967-5

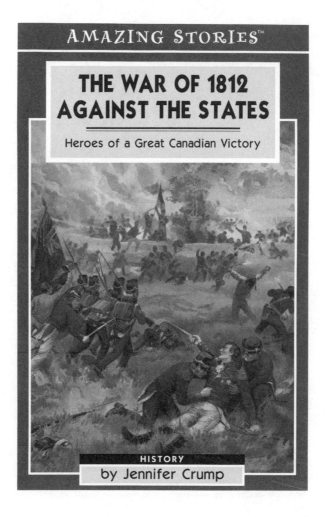

AMAZING STORIES™

THE WAR OF 1812 AGAINST THE STATES

Heroes of a Great Canadian Victory

HISTORY

by Jennifer Crump

ISBN 1-55153-948-9

OTHER AMAZING STORIES

ISBN	Title	Author
1-55153-962-3	British Columbia Murders	Susan McNicoll
1-55153-966-7	Canadian Spies	Tom Douglas
1-55153-982-9	Dinosaur Hunters	Lisa Murphy-Lamb
1-55153-970-5	Early Voyageurs	Marie Savage
1-55153-996-9	Emily Carr	Cat Klerks
1-55153-968-3	Edwin Alonzo Boyd	Nate Hendley
1-55153-961-6	Étienne Brûlé	Gail Douglas
1-55153-992-6	Ghost Town Stories II from the Red Coat Trail	Johnnie Bachusky
1-55153-973-X	Great Canadian Love Stories	Cheryl MacDonald
1-55153-946-2	Great Dog Stories	Roxanne Snopek
1-55153-958-6	Hudson's Bay Company Adventures	Elle Andra-Warner
1-55153-969-1	Klondike Joe Boyle	Stan Sauerwein
1-55153-967-5	Marie-Anne Lagimodiere	Irene Gordon
1-55153-964-0	Marilyn Bell	Patrick Tivy
1-55153-962-4	Niagara Daredevils	Cheryl MacDonald
1-55153-981-0	Rattenbury	Stan Sauerwein
1-55153-991-8	Rebel Women	Linda Kupecek
1-55153-995-0	Rescue Dogs	Dale Portman
1-55153-997-7	Sam Steele	Holly Quan
1-55153-954-3	Snowmobile Adventures	Linda Aksomitis
1-55153-986-1	Tales from the West Coast	Adrienne Mason
1-55153-950-0	Tom Thomson	Jim Poling Sr.
1-55153-976-4	Trailblazing Sports Heroes	Joan Dixon
1-55153-977-2	Unsung Heroes of the RCAF	Cynthia Faryon
1-55153-987-X	Wilderness Tales	Peter Christensen
1-55153-990-X	West Coast Adventures	Adrienne Mason
1-55153-948-9	War of 1812 Against the States	Jennifer Crump
1-55153-873-3	Women Explorers	Helen Y. Rolfe

These titles are available wherever you buy books. If you have trouble finding the book you want, call the Altitude order desk at 1-800-957-6888, e-mail your request to: orderdesk@altitudepublishing.com or visit our Web site at www.amazingstories.ca

New AMAZING STORIES titles are published every month. If you would like more information, e-mail your name and mailing address to: amazingstories@altitudepublishing.com.

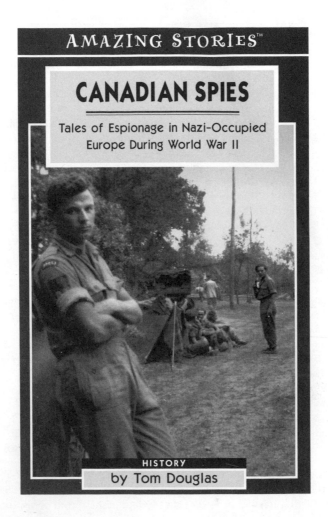

AMAZING STORIES™

CANADIAN SPIES

Tales of Espionage in Nazi-Occupied
Europe During World War II

HISTORY
by Tom Douglas

ISBN 1-55153-966-7